eB/paper 8x5, Embodying Aphrodite

A Sacred Path of Love, Sensual Alchemy & Divine Radiance

Sofia Hator

Contents

Acknowledgements

This book is dedicated to the Goddess in all her forms, seen and unseen, ancient and ever-living, and to the greatest good of all beings. May these words serve as a vessel of remembrance, healing, and awakening.

With deepest love and reverence, I offer a special thank you to my soul sister and spiral teacher, **Ur Mari Anna**. *Your presence has been a guiding light on this path, your wisdom a mirror to the divine.*

Blessings upon the sacred spiral we walk together.

Summoning

We have all heard the name Aphrodite, and we all know her as the goddess of love and beauty. Some of us even know her as the archetype of passion leading to creation and value that connects us to each other. All of these knowings stem from our predecessors, who carved her picture into marble and painted her image onto walls back in time in Greece and Italy, alongside the astrologies that have forged forth the learning of Venus.

For most of my life, I saw her as a Marilyn Monroe or Kim Kardashian archetype, admired for her beauty but often defined by it. I'll admit my bias, I've always been a fan of Kim. But my admiration isn't about her looks. It's her passion, relentless work ethic, and deep love for others,

especially her family, that stand out. More than anything, I respect her for following her own path, unapologetically pursuing what she loves.

What we see on the surface, without truly understanding what lies beneath, can create a complete misconception of someone's power and energy. Aphrodite may be the goddess of beauty, but she is also the goddess of creation.

My own bias toward her was shaped by naivety and conditioned by what I had seen but never truly explored for myself. Perhaps that is why she came to me, to reveal a hard truth about my own patterns of beauty, love, and self-worth. Through the journey of this book, I have come to know her not just as a symbol of beauty, but as a force that creates it, through inspiration, through the value we cultivate within ourselves and share with the world. It has been a profound shift in perspective.

I hope that as you move through these pages, you too will uncover more of her essence, so that together, we can carry her wisdom forward into the next evolution of human consciousness.

So, what is beauty? A rose is beautiful, not just in how it looks, but in how it smells, how it feels, and in the unspoken way it stirs something deep within us. It awakens a sensation that is difficult to name, yet intimately tied to the feeling of being alive, vibrant, enriched, and fully present in delicious ways. Beauty is more than what meets the eye, it reaches beyond the surface, activating all of our senses. And when every sense is awakened, it shifts us, pulling us beyond logic and into a state of superconsciousness, if only for a fleeting moment.

Working with Aphrodite's energy has revealed this truth to me. It has transformed my understanding of beauty from something seen to something felt, a force that creates, inspires, and elevates. My hope is that through this book, you too will experience this shift in perspective, seeing beauty not as a mere reflection, but as an activation, an opening of all your senses, and by extension, a pathway to the divine love of life itself.

Goddess work is my passion, and I feel deeply alive in this time of transformation, the great paradigm shift between the astrological ages of Pisces and Aquarius. And Aphrodite, I owe you an apology. I once bought into the illusion that you were merely a beautiful humanoid form, a reflection of surface-level admiration. How wrong I was to let that thought take root in my mindscape. Thank you for revealing your true essence, your light beyond the illusion.

Personal Invocation:

"As I write this book, invoking your energy and presence, I ask for compassionate guidance. Teach me to understand you, beauty, and love in their fullest, most holistic form, with depth, grace, and wisdom."

There is so much to uncover in Aphrodite's story. Even as I wrote, I found myself confronted with old wounds, revealing deeper layers of healing I hadn't expected. That is the nature of Goddess work, it transforms us. And in that transformation, I found myself, my path and for me that is through the act of writing, it allows me to dive deeper into her mysteries and to connect with Goddess more fully.

Aphrodite's future incarnations will be far more than a beautiful figure because she is evolving, expanding, becoming something even greater than she has ever been. I can't wait to see how creativity manifests in the mind of the greater collective as her image moves forward. A masterpiece is best shared, so if you feel inspired by her essence, connect with me on social media, I'd love to see your creations, your interpretations, and the ways her energy flows through you.

This is how love ripples outward, how beauty expands

beyond one soul and into the collective, igniting something new.

I also want to bring forth the idea that beauty is not confined to a woman's fertile years but extends into the wisdom of the crone, aged, wizened, and radiant in her own right. There is profound beauty in a life well-lived, in the stories woven into every wrinkle, in the grounding presence of those who have walked the path before us. They hold a kind of peace that only time can forge, offering a depth of love that is both expansive and enduring.

We must learn to see both faces, the youthful and the aged, and recognize them as reflections of the same truth: life is beautiful, and we honor that beauty through love. I want to witness love's essence shining through all forms of life, because I have come to know it, to recognize it in its many expressions. I want to see Aphrodite in all things, because she is in all things.

At its core, Aphrodite's energy is the love of life itself, the generative force that creates, sustains, and enriches existence. And when I speak of life, I do not mean a single individual's journey but the vast, interconnected experience of existence in its totality. Just as the ocean is not merely a collection of waves but a whole, living ecosystem, so too is Aphrodite's love, the energetic current that weaves together individual lives into a greater, harmonious whole.

This multidimensionality is key to expanding our perception. We can begin to understand Aphrodite's energy as both a force that shapes a single life over time and one that crafts an entire network of interconnected souls, just as the ocean, with all its creatures, currents, and tides, is both singular and infinite in its expression. This is the paradigm shift we are stepping into, the way of seeing that allows us to honor life in its fullest, most sacred form.

Archetypes are elusive things, like whispers of a deeper truth, always just beyond the grasp of logic.

Yesterday, I went to a football game, and as I watched the players warm up for their first match of the season, one caught my eye. He jogged over to the sideline, extending his hand to a friend, who responded with a handshake, a one-armed quick hug, and an easy smile. And in that simple exchange, something stirred in me, a rush of Aphrodite's energy.

In that moment, he was radiant with life. Present. Complete. Not because of status or skill, but because he was fully immersed in the energy of being, his joy, his presence, the love in that interaction. His entire being exuded a fullness, an aliveness that was undeniably beautiful.

I reflected on how he had arrived at this moment. The years of dedication, the unseen effort. The parents who had raised him, nurtured him, fed him, taught him. Every act of care and commitment had culminated in this, his moment of actualized love, the living essence of Aphrodite. She was not only in him but all around him, woven into the very architecture of that exchange, the moment, the history, movement, the joy. A reminder that Aphrodite's presence is not limited to romance or beauty but exists wherever life is fully embraced.

Aphrodite, as you will come to understand, is the goddess who existed before time itself, an eternal force of love and creation. She embodies the vibrational energy that manifests in countless ways, shaping and sustaining life. Deepening our understanding of her expands our awareness of who we are, what we create, and how we move through the world. Through her, we connect with others on a soul level, guided by reverence and gratitude. And it is through this kind of lived experience, one infused with love and presence, that we truly transform the world around us.

She is the essence we feel in the awe of a breathtaking sunset, in the serenity of merging with the ocean's embrace, in the quiet moments of emotional release where we become one with existence. To call upon her is to immerse yourself fully in life, to remember the beauty, to embody love, to allow her presence to inspire and heal. She soothes wounds of the heart, awakens deeper self-love, and teaches us to extend that love outward in its purest form.

But did you know that Aphrodite is also a Goddess of War?

At first, this may seem paradoxical, but within our earthly experience, all things exist in duality. Love is not only gentle and nourishing, it is also fierce, protective, and transformative. To honor Aphrodite's fullness, we must acknowledge both aspects of her nature. Only by embracing this duality can we move beyond the limitations of one-sided thinking, shedding the dogma that often breeds fear. Love, like life, is never static, it is a movement of creation and destruction, a dance between harmony and upheaval. And in understanding both sides of this sacred coin, we gain true integrity, wisdom, and power.

One of the most powerful realizations I've had through my spiritual practices, meditation, and High Priestess work is that society tends to teach only one half of the coin, perhaps only half of the truth of our 3D existence. This isn't necessarily done with malice. Intuitively, I sense it is more a reflection of our collective immaturity; as a species, we are still young, still learning.

Yet, the beauty we seek, the deep, fulfilling embodiment of love and creation, does not come without struggle. And to me, this struggle is the real war, the good war, the internal battle that pushes us to evolve, to break old patterns, to grow into our fullest expression. It is the force that challenges us, urges us forward, and ultimately transforms us. This is Aphrodite's war, the fight for love, for truth, not on the outside but within, it's the war to embrace the wholeness of life itself. If we consciously embrace our inner struggles, sit with them, and surrender to them, we find clarity.

As you journey deeper into this book, Aphrodite can be called upon to guide you through many inner realms, realms of creation and expression, as well as realms of surrender and receiving, all leading to healing. Healing and manifestation are two sides of the same coin, often used to describe the process of transformation. These words are everywhere right now because the energies are shifting, opening, and becoming more accessible. People are experiencing them with greater ease.

At its core, healing and manifestation are simply the natural rhythm of life. When we give and receive in harmony, we allow each person to be uniquely themselves while remaining deeply connected to the whole. This is my wish for the Aquarian Age, that we move with this rhythm, embracing both our individuality and our unity with grace.

We have always been manifestors. As human beings, creation is woven into our very essence. It is an extension of our inner being into the material world, the reason we are here. Through what we create, we experience life and time, we cultivate connection and unconditional love, and we leave our imprint on existence, learning, evolving, and discovering who we truly are.

Interconnectedness is another essential aspect of Aphrodite's wisdom, one you will see throughout this book. It is not only through our relationships but also through the sharing of our creations, our inner experiences, and our love that we connect with something greater than ourselves. Aphrodite reminds us that beauty, love, and creation are never solitary endeavors. They are forces that ripple outward, binding us to each other, to life, and to the divine.

Through this book, we invoke Aphrodite to explore the pathways she has laid before us, opening ourselves to receive love, from the cosmos, from ourselves, and from others. She supports the birth of our dreams and desires, not through force, but through the transformative power of true love and alignment with the universe.

Desire is simply a call to create, a sacred pull toward something essential. What we truly desire, we also need, for it is through desire that we grow and heal. In goddess work, the call to transformation is undeniable. When we journey deep within, we already know how to heal ourselves, right down to our fundamental energetic core. This is sacred work.

Our desires are deeply connected to our life's purpose and naturally evolve as we do. As we expand, our desires shift, revealing deeper truths. At first, we may think we desire something material, such as a million dollars. But as we move toward it, we realize our true longing was never for the number itself but for what it represents, security, freedom, a thriving home for our family. The monetary figure was merely symbolic. When we reach this awareness, we gain liberation through growth. Over time, this process leads to a state beyond longing, self-actualization.

I have a humorous personal story about this. During one phase of my spiritual awakening, I reached a point where I genuinely desired nothing. I had everything I needed. Life felt whole, complete. The only problem? I had no motivation. I found myself wondering, Why even get dressed today if I'm just going to put my pajamas back on in a few hours? It made absolutely no sense, and in that state, life begins to unravel.

Desire, then, is not something to suppress or fear, it is a force that moves us forward, that keeps us engaged with the unfolding journey of life itself. Long story short, I remember telling the universe, Goddess, God, all that is, I choose to stay. Please give me something meaningful to do because I no longer know what to do. And of course, here I am, writing these books.

I share this story to illustrate that desire isn't inherently bad; it is woven into existence. It only becomes destructive when twisted into something harmful. But if you trust yourself, then the path forward is only up. Even if you stumble, your mistakes will become a part of your growth.

Recognizing Aphrodite's connection to desire as a guidepost on our life's journey, and a way to consciously know ourselves. The freedom to grow, explore, and create through manifestation becomes accessible with this knowledge. So let your desire be an invitation to joy, to play, to reveal yourself to yourself in the adventure of being human.

Call upon Aphrodite as you journey through this book. Ask her to ease your way into higher vibrations of beauty, love, and expression. Her energy will uplift you, surrounding you with the quiet yet powerful magic that is always present. Open to her blessings, for when we enter the natural flow of giving and receiving, we have more ease and less exhaustion.

Call out to her now. Say into the open space before you: *"I invoke Aphrodite, holy mentor, to reinvigorate me and show me the way of self-love."*

Now, say it again, either aloud or within your being, but this time, truly feel the resonance. Speak with meaning. Let the energy of the words wash over you like a prayer. Sense their vibration moving through your body, expanding outward into the collective consciousness.

When I was nearing the completion of this book, I unexpectedly spent four days in the hospital. My sister had strongly urged me to visit the Emergency Department, and on the very day I was admitted, the Venus star point went into retrograde (I'll explore star points later). Yet, despite the circumstances, I remained centered in love and positivity, deeply anchored in Aphrodite's energy. Alone in that hospital room, I felt no fear. I rested, I slept, and I continued my work with purpose.

Six days later, I embarked on an inner journey, following the ancient path of Inanna's descent to her sister Ereshkigal, the path of quiet transformation. Walking this priestess pathway shifted something profound within me, particularly around the balance of giving and receiving. Yet, like all sacred work, this journey is ongoing, still unfolding in its own time.

For now, let us turn our gaze backward. Let us look at her story, Aphrodite's origins, so that we may deepen our understanding of this powerful goddess archetype and all that she has to teach us.

Herstory

Aphrodite, the goddess renowned for her beauty, is often depicted in art and literature as the most breathtaking woman to have ever graced the earth. But this perception captures only a fraction of her true essence. Her form is more than an aesthetic ideal; it symbolizes something far more profound. In energetic terms, Aphrodite embodies a vibration that draws attention, sparks inspiration, and awakens the extraordinary into motion.

Take a moment now, close your eyes and think about beauty. Then shift from thinking about beauty to feeling it. Do you notice the shift? As we transition into the Age of Aquarius, more of us are beginning to experience beauty not just as a concept, but as an energy. Try to put words to this feeling. How would you describe it? This exercise helps re-pattern conditioned beliefs about what has been ingrained in us as "beauty." Naming this feeling can be challenging because archetypes, by their nature, are elusive, too vast to be confined to a single definition.

If you resonate with my experience, you may recognize that true beauty surpasses the physical. It becomes something divine, even orgasmic, not in the literal sense, but as a full-bodied, life-affirming experience. It is the difference between simply admiring an object and feeling its presence stir something deep within, opening you to love and connection. From here, Aphrodite's link to fertility becomes clear.

As we explore her historical timeline, her herstory, it's essential to first understand fertility beyond its common association with biological reproduction. Fertility is a sacral-chakra force, the power of creation itself. To limit it to childbirth is to overlook its vast potential. We, as humans, embody this energy in countless ways, raising a family is one form, but so is art. Art is the active process of drawing forth inner visions and shaping them into reality. It thrives in advanced civilizations and flourishes when the collective consciousness aligns with creation.

Art births new ideas, new perspectives, and sometimes entire cultural revolutions.

But art is not limited to painting or sculpture. It is a boundless creative expression. You taste it in an exquisitely crafted meal, feel it in a home infused with warmth and love, hear it in music that moves your soul. Even these words, as I write them, flow from a place beyond structured thought, they are channeled. This, too, is art.

Yoga is another form of art, rooted in presence, movement, and connection to the divine. It evokes a feeling that is difficult to name but effortless to experience. We are drawn to it, just as we are drawn to all things that sustain life, kindness, love, beauty, and creation itself. This divine, artful presence is the true essence of Aphrodite. She is not just a goddess of love, but of creative abundance, showing us that life can be graceful and rich when we align with our innate ability to manifest.

The Birth of Aphrodite

The first place most people think of when they hear the name Aphrodite is Greek mythology. However, archaeological evidence suggests that the worship of a fertility goddess on Cyprus predates the Greek identification of Aphrodite by millennia. As early as 3800 BCE, sites in the Paphos region, such as Kouklia-Vathyrkakas, Lemba, and Kissonerga, reveal the presence of a cult devoted to a powerful mother goddess associated with fertility and nature.

Early rituals honoring this divine feminine force likely involved offerings and ceremonies meant to celebrate the life-giving forces of nature. These rites would have centered on abundance, gratitude, and the cycles of creation. The idea that her early worship required blood sacrifice does not align with her life-affirming essence. Ancient artifacts, such as figurines depicting the feminine form with pronounced features symbolizing fertility, ceremonial altars, and votive offerings, suggest a reverence for the goddess as a nurturing, life-giving presence.

The transformation of this local fertility goddess into the Hellenic Aphrodite was shaped by Cyprus's position as a cultural crossroads. The island, strategically located along Mediterranean trade routes, became a melting pot of religious traditions, influenced by the Phoenicians, Egyptians, and Greeks. Among these influences was Astarte, the Phoenician goddess of love, fertility, and sovereignty, whose attributes closely mirrored those of the Cypriot goddess. Through cultural blending, Aphrodite emerged as a synthesis of these divine archetypes, absorbing aspects of Astarte's power into her own identity.

It is beautifully fitting that Aphrodite, a goddess of fertility and creation, was herself born from the cultural fusion of multiple civilizations. Through this exchange, a renewed and expanded motif of Aphrodite emerged, one that reflects the very essence of what she represents: life-giving creativity, growth, and harmonious union.

By the time of Homer (800 BCE), Aphrodite was firmly established as a major deity in Cyprus, with Paphos recognized as her most sacred cult center. Homer describes her sanctuary as an altar fragrant with incense, where she was bathed and anointed by the Graces. The Sanctuary of Aphrodite Paphia in Paphos, unlike later Greco-Roman temples, featured an open-air design, reinforcing its deep connection to nature. Central to this worship was a conical stone, believed to represent the goddess herself, around which rituals were performed.

In Greek history, two primary myths recount Aphrodite's birth, recorded between the 8th and 7th centuries BCE.

The Theogony (written around 700 BCE) presents a dramatic version of the classic father-versus-son struggle, a story that has echoed throughout mythology. According to this tale, Aphrodite was born from this feud when Cronus (the son) overthrew Uranus (his father, the sky god), casting his severed genitals into the sea. From the foaming waters, Aphrodite emerged, fully formed and astonishingly beautiful.

I suppose that's one way for males to create life.

The Theogony myth continues with Aphrodite arriving near the island of Cythera before drifting to Cyprus, where she came ashore at Paphos. This story establishes Cyprus, and specifically Paphos, as her sacred birthplace, intertwining her identity with the island's geography and culture. Though I have never been to Paphos, I imagine its stories and folklore are rich with magic, deeply rooted in the land's fertility and beauty. Perhaps one day, I will go and see for myself.

The second place Aphrodite's birth is mentioned is in Homer's Iliad (written around 750–700 BCE), where she is described as the daughter of Zeus and the Titaness Dione. Unlike the dramatic and cosmic origins recounted in Theogony, this version presents Aphrodite as a more conventional Olympian deity, born through divine lineage rather than an act of celestial upheaval.

This alternate genealogy ties Aphrodite more closely to the Olympian pantheon, aligning her with Zeus and the other major gods rather than portraying her as an ancient, primordial force. However, despite this differing origin story, both versions highlight her immense power and enduring influence as a goddess of love, beauty, and desire.

Historical texts mention sacrifices to Aphrodite, but these accounts require closer examination. Offerings such as incense, grains, and other life-affirming gifts align naturally with the goddess's themes of abundance and prosperity. However, the claim that animal sacrifices, especially the sacrifice of doves, were part of her rites is one I deeply question. Later in this book, I will explore this topic further, drawing on both historical sources and my own intuitive insights to challenge prevailing narratives about Aphrodite's worship.

At the heart of the Sanctuary of Aphrodite Paphia in Paphos stood a sacred conical stone, representing the goddess herself. Devotees gathered here to offer sacrifices, with historical sources mentioning incense, grains, and, according to some accounts, animals. While the symbolic offerings of incense and grains, representing gratitude and abundance, align with Aphrodite's essence, I question whether animal sacrifice was ever truly part of her ancient rites. Later in this book, I will examine this further, considering both historical records and spiritual insight to reassess these claims.

Archaeological evidence suggests that the worship of a powerful mother goddess in Cyprus dates back to at least 3800 BCE, long before the Hellenistic era. Sites such as Kouklia-Vathyrkakas, Lemba, and Kissonerga reveal a deep-rooted reverence for a fertility goddess intricately connected to nature. This challenges the Greek mythological narrative that Aphrodite was born from the severed genitals of Uranus, a story that frames her existence as a consequence of male conflict. In truth, she was never created through an act of violence; rather, she had always been present, fully actualized as a divine force of creation and life.

Aphrodite's story is not merely one of beauty and love, it is a testament to spiritual transformation, cultural fusion, and the enduring power of the divine feminine. Through her evolving presence, we witness how civilizations interact, blend, and redefine their understanding of the sacred. She is, herself, an embodiment of creative synergy and divine interconnectedness.

The Sanctuary of Aphrodite Paphia became the epicenter of her worship. Unlike the enclosed temples that later characterized Greco-Roman religious structures, this sanctuary maintained an open-air design, reflecting an ancient Oriental influence that emphasized a deep connection with nature. At its center stood a conical stone, believed to symbolize the goddess herself, around which rituals were performed. Historical sources describe devotees offering incense, grains, and, in some accounts, animals, as tributes to honor Aphrodite.

However, while incense and grains align with themes of abundance and gratitude, I challenge the conventional assumption that animal sacrifice, particularly the sacrifice of doves, was a fundamental part of her worship. Later in this book, I will explore this topic further, analyzing historical records and intuitive insights to reconsider whether these rituals were truly integral to her cult or whether they were later impositions influenced by shifting cultural and religious landscapes.

One of the most significant celebrations in her honor was the Aphrodisia festival, held in midsummer to honor Aphrodite's divine presence. The very name Aphrodisia, meaning "pertaining to Aphrodite" or "sacred to Aphrodite", reveals the depth of her influence on ancient society. Over time, this term evolved into aphrodisiac, meaning something that stimulates love or desire. This linguistic shift reflects how patriarchal recontextualization reduced Aphrodite's archetype, stripping away the complexity of her role and leaving behind a narrow, sensual interpretation of desire. In reality, her essence encompassed a much broader spectrum of love, harmony, and creative life force.

It is also worth reconsidering the widely accepted etymology of her name. The traditional explanation links Aphrodite to aphros (ἀφρός), meaning "sea foam," reinforcing the myth of her oceanic birth. However, modern scholars regard this as folk etymology, an informal interpretation lacking linguistic rigor. Instead, research suggests that her name may be of non-Greek, possibly Semitic origin, aligning with theories that connect her to the Phoenician goddess Astarte. Alternative hypotheses propose an Indo-European linguistic connection, with some scholars suggesting her name derives from words meaning "bright" or "shining," potentially linking her to celestial light or dawn deities. This supports the idea that her divine essence was originally connected to fertility, renewal, and cosmic harmony, rather than being solely associated with romantic or sensual love.

The Aphrodisia festival was celebrated across Greece, Cyprus, and the broader Mediterranean, with each region incorporating unique traditions. It served as both a public and private act of devotion, fostering communal bonds through processions, music, and sacred dances performed in Aphrodite's groves throughout the countryside.

In Athens, worshippers gathered at the Sanctuary of Aphrodite Pandemos and Peitho, located on the southwestern slopes of the Acropolis. Amidst the grandeur of marble structures and the bustling energy of the city, rituals commenced with the purification of the temple. Doves, sacred to Aphrodite, I discovered to beat their wings to cleanse the air, a ritual I find far more symbolically fitting than the widely accepted notion of blood sacrifice.

Later in this book, I will challenge archaeological interpretations that assume the presence of sacrificial doves in Aphrodite's rites, offering a perspective that aligns more closely with her life-affirming nature.

Through this exploration, I hope to restore a more nuanced and accurate understanding of Aphrodite as a goddess of love, creativity, and spiritual transformation, rather than merely a figure associated with sensual pleasure.

After the purification rituals, sacred images of Aphrodite and her companion goddess Peitho, the goddess of persuasion and attraction, were carried through the streets in grand processions, eventually reaching the sea for ceremonial washing. This ritual, symbolizing renewal and divine reverence, reflected Aphrodite's connection to water, purification, and cyclical rebirth. In Corinth, Aphrodite's worship took on a different expression. The city's renowned hetairai, female companions and courtesans, became deeply intertwined with the festival, emphasizing her role as the goddess of beauty, love, and pleasure. Unlike later moralistic interpretations of courtesanship, in ancient times, hetairai were highly educated women, skilled in conversation, music, and the arts, often holding positions of considerable influence. Their presence within Aphrodite's worship highlights her as a patroness of sacred sensuality, attraction, and the power of feminine allure in all its forms.

However, in rural areas and on the islands, the

celebrations were even wilder. In Cyprus, particularly in Paphos, the Aphrodisia festival was celebrated with great fervor. Worshippers gathered in Aphrodite's temples and sacred groves, offering local produce and performing rituals deeply connected to fertility and the natural world. Ritual bathing in the sea symbolized renewal, while ceremonial dances invoked growth and transformation. Communal feasts featuring foods linked to abundance and prosperity reinforced the connection between Aphrodite and the cycles of life. These practices reveal Aphrodite's presence as more than a goddess of love, she was a force of sovereignty, creation, and divine magnetism.

This reminds me of a festival I once attended in Scotland, the Beltane Fire Festival atop Calton Hill in Edinburgh. Beltane, an ancient Gaelic festival marking the awakening of summer, fertility, and passion, resonates deeply with Aphrodite's themes. That night, the air pulsed with raw energy. Observers stood spellbound, encircling the sacred space, watching as the May Queen and the Green Man, embodiments of fertility and desire, performed the rites. The celebration unfolded in hypnotic rhythms of drums, dancing, and bodies painted in vivid colors, moving as one in an ancient, primal dance of renewal. The sensuality of the ritual was not merely physical, it was spiritual, ecstatic, and transformative. Watching it unfold, I was reminded that the energy of love, creation, and divine feminine power is timeless. It has been celebrated for millennia, under many names, across many lands.

Rituals dedicated to Aphrodite in Cyprus were diverse and evolved over time, reflecting her multifaceted nature. Ancient records describe offerings of incense, flowers, and crafted items to seek her favor. Ceremonial purifications, bathing in the sea or sacred pools, emulated her mythical sea birth, while annual festivals aligned with agricultural cycles, featuring processions, music, and sacred dances. However, one claim that has long troubled me is the supposed sacrifice of doves in Aphrodite's name. The goddess's energy rejected this notion, compelling me to pause my writing and enter deep meditation. I was apprehensive, what if I found evidence that blood sacrifice had been part of her rites?

Before meditating, I turned to historical research, determined to uncover the truth. Upon reviewing primary sources, I found no direct evidence that Aphrodite's followers practiced dove sacrifice. Even on Wikipedia, there were no references to ancient texts documenting dove blood purification rituals.

Erika Simon's Festivals of Attica: An Archaeological Companion discusses rituals associated with Aphrodite but does not cite primary sources on dove sacrifice. Similarly, Pausanias' Description of Greece, which offers extensive insights into Greek religious practices, does not mention this ritual. Given the absence of direct citations, it's likely that this practice was either a later misinterpretation or a symbolic sacrifice that was misunderstood as literal. And this realization aligns with what my intuition was already telling me.

When I entered meditation, the first message that came through was that the festival was not called Aphrodisia, it was the Festival of Light and Love. Immediately, I researched this and discovered Lychnapsia, an ancient Festival of Lights celebrated on August 12 in honor of the Egyptian goddess Isis, whose worship spread to Greece. Participants illuminated their surroundings with lamps, symbolizing enlightenment, transformation, and the dispelling of darkness, a theme deeply resonant with Aphrodite's path. Then, another phrase resonated within me: "I worship her hair. I worship her, She who continues the work of her predecessor." Words alone cannot capture the vibrational depth of this message. Alongside these words, I received a vision, a sacred vow, a chant of devotion to feminine energy in all its forms.

Aphrodite's essence pulsed through the vision. "I worship the form of Woman incarnate. The cycles of creation. You, the woman, honor this archetype within yourself. Honor the Feminine in all her expressions." This was not worship in the sense of mere adoration, it was a sacred honoring of the life-giving force of the Feminine, the custodianship of creation itself. And with this came another truth. The doves were never sacrificed. They were brought forth at the beginning of the festival. Their wings beat in rhythmic offering, lifting away stagnant energy, cleansing the space. When their work was done, they were placed at the four corners of the sacred space, living sentinels of divine energy.

And so, when the women arrived, dancing, crying, releasing, they stepped into a space of transformation. They invoked the Devoted Mother, the Unashamed Lover, the Peaceful Warrior, the Surrendered Flower. They let go of their old selves. This was the sacrifice, not of flesh, but of fear, doubt, and limitation. Aphrodite does not demand blood, she guides us to shed what no longer serves. And so, when the final dance settled into stillness, the women wove their blankets around themselves, cocooning in self-renewal. They poured libations, to the earth, to themselves, to the endless cycle of life. And they were reborn.

This revelation reshapes my understanding of Aphrodite's worship. She was never merely a goddess of romantic love, she was a guardian of renewal, transformation, and feminine sovereignty. The Festival of Light and Love was a celebration of the divine feminine in all its forms. And in this space, there was no sacrifice of flesh, only the surrender of fear. Aphrodite guides us still. She whispers: Let go. Transform. Become. And this, dear reader, is her true essence.

Encoded

To truly understand Aphrodite's essence, we must look beyond the well-known accounts of Theogony and The Iliad and journey far back, before the Greek pantheon, before recorded myth, to the ancient civilizations that revered her predecessors. Myths are not static; they are retellings of sacred truths, shaped and reshaped over time to align with the shifting consciousness of each astrological age. Aphrodite's story is no different.

Approximately 3,000 years before Hesiod and Homer, goddesses of fertility, love, and creation were already venerated in the ancient Near East. These powerful deities influenced the Aphrodite we recognize today, bridging cultures and spiritual traditions across vast stretches of time.

Aphrodite's lineage can be traced through a succession of ancient Goddesses, Inanna of Sumer, Ishtar of Akkad, and Astarte of Phoenicia. Inanna, a goddess of love, beauty, sexuality, fertility, and war, was known for her transformational myths, many of which emphasized power, death, and rebirth. Ishtar retained these themes, embodying the duality of nurturer and warrior. Astarte, too, was a goddess of fertility, sovereignty, and sacred sexuality, often depicted with symbols of divine authority.

A fascinating book, The Lost Gospel by Simcha Jacobovici and Barrie Wilson, explores the evolution of divine feminine worship and its echoes in early Christianity. The book reveals a hidden document suggesting that Mary Magdalene and Jesus were not only married but also served as a living embodiment of the spiritual consciousness of the Age of Pisces. This interpretation draws a direct link between the goddess traditions of Astarte and the eventual veneration of Mary Magdalene, positioning her as a continuation of the divine feminine lineage. More than a disciple, she emerges as a vessel of ancient priestess wisdom, carrying forward esoteric teachings long encoded within sacred traditions.

It is a book that challenges perception, expanding the lens through which we view history, spirituality, and the ways sacred knowledge has been preserved through time. It also reveals how goddess-worshipping cultures transitioned into patriarchal religious structures, shaping the world we now inhabit. If you seek to reclaim the lost threads of divine feminine wisdom, this book is a compelling place to start.

The goddesses that preceded Aphrodite all carried aspects of love, fertility, and war, a reflection of the ancients' understanding of creation and destruction as inseparable forces. Today, we still struggle with this concept, conditioned to see life in binary terms rather than cyclical ones. Ancient peoples, deeply attuned to nature, understood that life was to be lived, loved, and surrendered to. The rhythms of the seasons and the waxing and waning of the moon were constant reminders of this truth.

This understanding was once embedded in the way Aphrodite was perceived. Yet, over time, we have forgotten that she is not only the goddess of love and beauty but also of war. Not war in the sense of external battles, but the internal struggle, the war between fear and surrender, between the desire to say yes and the impulse to say no. I won't attempt to generalize what this means for each person, as every journey is unique, but it is important to recognize that this inner war is natural. It is part of the unfolding process of self-realization.

That, in essence, is the good war, the battle that leads to growth, to clarity, to transformation.

But would you believe me if I told you that this is not where Aphrodite's story begins? The goddess's origins extend far beyond Mesopotamian history, deep into the prehistoric past. While this period is less clearly defined, scholars believe that proto-goddesses existed in Neolithic and early Bronze Age societies, long before recorded myth.

Perhaps the story begins around 30,000 BCE, in an era when Asherah was known as the Tree of Life, a divine force representing the feminine power within creation. The people of this time carved and treasured what we now call Venus figurines, though to them, these artifacts were likely sacred representations of the moon's cycles and the mysteries of birth, life, and death.

These were the times of small, nomadic tribes, moving

in rhythm with the land. Nature was everything, teacher, protector, sustainer, and the divine feminine was honored as the embodiment of this force. The Venus figurines found across Europe from this period reveal a long-standing reverence for the female form as a source of nourishment, life, and power. This makes sense, as it was a fundamental truth, without the feminine force, there was no future, no continuation of existence.

As time passed, human societies became more structured, and so too did their mythology. Around 7000 BCE, as nomadic tribes settled into agrarian communities, the goddess evolved into a distinct Prehistoric Mother figure, still deeply tied to fertility but now also representing agriculture, protection, and the sustenance of settled life.

By 4000 BCE, with the rise of Mesopotamian civilization, she emerged as Ninhursag, the Great Mother of the Gods. Closely linked to agriculture, midwifery, and childbirth, she was honored as a primordial mother who birthed the divine. Her mythology reflected the shift from nomadic existence to the stability of farming, marking another major transformation in human consciousness.

In 3500 BCE, she took on another form, Nisaba, goddess of grain and wisdom. Her presence deepened into the realm of sacred knowledge, particularly in connection to women's wisdom and earth's abundance. This was the period in which writing was introduced through patterns and symbols, marking yet another shift in human understanding. Nisaba's association with both fertility and literacy highlights the connection between creativity and communication, an idea that would carry forward into later goddess traditions.

Then came Inanna, Ishtar, and Astarte, each a refinement of the same essential force, until finally, she became Aphrodite. And later still, the Romans called her Venus. But her story did not end there.

By 200 CE, as Christianity rose to dominance, the goddess's worship began to fade. Astarte's temples were abandoned, Aphrodite's rituals ceased, and the sacred feminine was rebranded into new figures. And yet, she remained, her presence now split, appearing as Mary Magdalene and Mother Mary, fragmented yet ever-present. That split, of course, is a story for another time.

But here's what I know. No matter what we call her, Aphrodite, Venus, Astarte, Mary, she has never left us. She is woven into the fabric of our stories, into the wisdom passed from generation to generation. The myths may change, the names may shift, but the divine feminine is eternal. She is, and always will be, with us.

I have included a timeline of Goddess worship with corresponding astrological ages in a table format for easy reference. Just note that you could probably add many other goddess names to this list, I just haven't done the research. My goal was simply to give you the general gist of the timeline of this love vibration, which stretches all the way back before her recent Greek storyline.

Timeline of Goddess Worship with Corresponding Astrological Ages

Goddess	Civilization	Worship Period (BCE)	Associations	Astrological Age
Prehistoric Mother Goddess	Prehistoric cultures (Ubaid, Halaf, etc.)	7000–4000 BCE	Life, fertility, nature	Age of Gemini / Age of Taurus
Ninhursag (Mother of the Gods)	Sumerian	4000–2500 BCE	Earth, birth, nurturing	Age of Taurus / Age of Aries
Nisaba (Goddess of Grain & Wisdom)	Sumerian	3500–2000 BCE	Knowledge, writing, abundance	Age of Taurus / Age of Aries
Asherah (Proto-Canaanite)	Canaanite/Semitic	3000–1000 BCE	Tree of Life, creation, fertility	Age of Aries
Inanna	Sumerian (Uruk)	4000–2000 BCE	Love, war, power, celestial forces	Age of Taurus / Age of Aries
Ishtar	Akkadian/Babylonian	2000–600 BCE	Love, war, fertility, sexuality	Age of Aries
Astarte	Phoenician/Canaanite	1800 BCE–200 CE	Love, war, sailors, protection	Age of Aries / Age of Pisces
Aphrodite	Greek	1200–500 BCE	Love, beauty, desire, harmony	Age of Pisces

Archetypes

Aphrodite reveals herself in many faces, each a reflection of the divine feminine's depth and complexity. Before we explore these sacred expressions, we must first understand the essence of psychology, not as a rigid structure that we need to conform to inside the mind, but as a fluid and evolving journey of the soul. Psychology, in its truest form, is the language of the inner world, a map of the emotions, instincts, and archetypes that shape our existence. It actually hasn't been around for that long, so this map is fairly small and doesn't contain the complexities that will come over time and through expanded consciousness. But it is a map nevertheless, and so it can help us to see ourselves and reduce some of the fear we may have of ourselves.

As a study of behavior, psychology offers a peek behind the curtains of the dance between the seen and unseen world we all have. Each person is different, and so psychology offers a contextual framework to better know the conscious and unconscious, the light and shadow, and the workings of transformation at play in each person's life. But it is necessary to realize that because of the differences of each person in each moment, this map of psychology is both ever-growing and evolving and, at the same time, fluid from an individual perspective's framework.

With that being said, the approach of psychology is to use it to understand ourselves, not as something fixed, but as something ever-changing, shaped by experience, perception, and the depths of our inner world. We don't need to confine or label ourselves and our parts with this tool, but rather use it as a guide to illuminate the unseen pathways within us, offering insights into why we feel, act, and react the way we do. When approached with openness, psychology allows us to navigate the complexities of our inner world with greater awareness, helping us integrate both our wounds and our wisdom.

Sadhguru, a modern mystic and spiritual teacher, offers a profound perspective on psychology, reminding us that true understanding of the mind goes beyond intellectual analysis. He speaks of the mind as a vast and complex mechanism, shaped by past impressions, conditioning, and unconscious tendencies. The mind, in its current state, largely focuses on memory and perception, but it does not yet fully account for the boundless nature of human consciousness. He emphasizes that transformation cannot happen merely by understanding the patterns of the mind; it requires a shift in inner experience, which is where meditation comes in to shift realities. In my experience, this is exactly what meditation does. It opens one individual human perspective to a greater consciousness, and oh, the stories I could tell. In fact, it is through this consciousness doorway that I now have the ability to channel.

In Sadhguru's teachings, psychology is useful to the extent that it helps us see our own unconscious patterns, but it is not the destination, it is only a tool. True well-being and freedom arise when we recognize that we are not our thoughts, emotions, or past experiences, but something far beyond them. He encourages us to use psychology not as a means to define ourselves, but as a stepping stone toward a deeper spiritual awareness. In this way, psychology can assist us in dissolving limitations and breaking free from repetitive cycles of suffering, allowing us to step into a state of clarity, joy, and inner expansiveness.

If you want to know your psychological patterns, you only need to start meditating. They are there on repeat when you sit quietly and turn inwards. In my experience, most people say, "I cannot meditate, my mind is too active." But what they are really saying is that it is so annoying to sit there and see themselves, they would rather pretend that the loud, repetitive voice can be ignored, and we all know what that leads to.

So bringing this wisdom back to Aphrodite, we see that she is not simply a psychological construct of a bunch of archetypal roles to be studied, she is a living, breathing force of transformation. In a way, we can think of her energy as that which can push open the doorway between a pattern we are running in our consciousness and unconsciousness and into the vast superconscious realms of light.

Because she embodies love, we can hold her energy as we sit in meditation or mindfulness practices like rituals, to help bridge that compassionate gap between wanting to heal and integrate and seeing ourselves for how we truly are in that moment. She can soothe the shatters within and reveal truth beneath illusion. She actually urges us to see our patterns, so we can remove the trappings and transmute them into something greater. To work with her is to step beyond intellectual understanding and into deep, embodied experience. It is to trust the dance of the unseen, to surrender to the wisdom of the heart, and to embrace the divine feminine's unfolding journey through us.

Aphrodite's essence, through this lens, is to embrace the wisdom that she is not one thing but many. She is love, beauty, pleasure, and passion, and these things exist within her essence to transform, from chaos to sacredness, that which is within. She does not fit into a single definition, nor does she belong to only one archetype. Instead, she weaves between them, embodying the wholeness of the feminine in all her radiant, untamed, and ever-changing glory.

As we walk this path, let us remember that understanding Aphrodite is not about categorizing her, nor is it about forcing her into the confines of traditional psychology. It is about allowing her to reveal herself in ways that awaken us, challenge us, and return us to our own sacred knowing. In doing so, we do not merely study her, we become her.

Aphrodite's archetypes are the Lover, Muse, Healer, Warrior, and Creator of Worlds. Through these archetypes, we weave together historical interpretations and psychological insights to better understand her influence on the human experience. As the Lover, she teaches the value of connection and passion. As the Muse, she inspires creativity and self-expression. As the Healer, she guides emotional transformation. As the Warrior, she represents the power to stand in the "good fight" and trust the process of evolution, ensuring internal and external growth. And as the Creator of Worlds, she embodies fertility, not just of life but of entire ecosystems, relationships, and realities, all woven from love.

Understanding these aspects deepens our ability to work with Aphrodite energetically, allowing us to invoke her presence with intention. When we call upon her, we are not summoning something outside of ourselves, we are activating parts of our own being.

The Lover

Aphrodite's Lover aspect connects us to our emotions, physicality, and the pursuit of beauty, not just in appearance, but in our experience of life. This face of aphrodite reminds us of the grace that exists in all things, from intimate relationships to the joy of community and the sense of belonging. Carl Jung thinks of the Lover as one of the primary archetypes that influence human behavior. From birth, we experience the love of family and kinship which in turn make us strong and individual. As we grow, we long reform that connection, seeking our tribe and our place in the world. Then in our elder years, we become holders of sacred space, passing on the legacies of love and wisdom to the next generation. The overarching love is a foundational principle to human life and it is one we are always looking to be fulfilled with.

Jung's research suggests that embracing the Lover archetype allows harmony to flow more easily, helping individuals live without fear and create from a place of emotional depth. And we can do this by letting go of our beliefs being pressed upon others through the practice of meditation and opening up to unconditional love.

My experience with opening to unconditional love stems from my spiritual awakening, where my heart chakra burst open, and all of a sudden, I could feel vibrations all the time. I now know this is my personal style of language, and I am still, and I guess will always be, in a state of learning the language of vibrations. But it was through meditation, divine timing, and allowing myself to surrender that the experience unfolded in its entirety. It took years, actually, and has left me with a positioning of unconditional love for all and a deep compassion for every being, creature, and life itself.

Jung also warned of the Lover's shadowy side, which is an over-identification with another, leading to dependency or a loss of self. We see this reflected in the way societal narratives shape our understanding of love and even in the stories we consume through books, movies, and media. Often, we absorb the stories we are told about relationships, regurgitating old ideals without questioning their truth, like the trope of "you complete me," where love is portrayed as finding another person to fill a perceived void within ourselves. This idea, seen in countless romance films and novels, suggests that we are incomplete without a partner, reinforcing emotional dependence rather than self-fulfillment.

But Aphrodite teaches us to love with fresh eyes, to carve our own paths in connection within ourselves. The new narrative is that we complete ourselves, and, in truth, we have had that power all along. Love, in its highest form, is not about seeking wholeness in another but recognizing the wholeness already within us. When we honor our individual experiences, we evolve naturally, rather than clinging to outdated structures that create pain and conflict. By embracing this truth, we step into love as a conscious choice, one rooted in self-awareness, freedom, and genuine connection rather than unconscious longing or external validation.

Robert A. Johnson, in She: Understanding Feminine Psychology, explores the Lover archetype and emphasizes the importance of balancing this energy. He highlights the need to cultivate love without losing autonomy, a lesson that is echoed in Jean Shinoda Bolen's Goddesses in Everywoman.

A modern narrative that needs work is the recurring trope in which the female or feminine point of view loses autonomy through falling in love, and we see the echoes of this in many stories. It is interesting to note that when women have children, or, in fact, when anyone becomes a parent, autonomy is somewhat given over in order to raise a child. And yet, it is important to keep that autonomy within our being so that we can show our children that we can hold differences and nuances in love, allowing them to carry the structural architecture of previous societies a little more loosely and with less rigidity.

The Muse

Beyond love, Aphrodite is the Muse, a divine force that fuels artistic inspiration. How she does this is very interesting because she is like fuel and, at the same time, the spark. She is the current that moves through poets, painters, musicians, and visionaries, urging them to bring their inner worlds into form, but also the sustainer that completes the masterpiece because of the value it holds in its expression and the reverence of those who come in contact with the piece. We all know this because the music of Beethoven, even to this day, still creates feelings of love and passion within the listener.

Aphrodite is often thought of as a fertile goddess, and it is through this expression of creativity, of being ignited and then creating with the essence of love and value, that she shows us fertility is the creation of form in life. This book, in its essence, is a reflection of that very energy. Writing it has often felt like being overtaken by something greater than myself, as if I were merely a vessel through which words flowed. This is what it means to be in the Muse's embrace, to surrender to creation.

Psychologically, the Muse represents the source of inspiration that drives individuals toward self-expression and, ultimately, self-actualization. Engaging with this aspect of Aphrodite leads to profound personal growth, as it encourages us to explore our inner world and articulate unique perspectives. Our lives themselves become works of art, shaped by our choices, emotions, and perceptions.

In ancient times, poets and artists invoked Aphrodite to awaken the Muse within, believing that her presence could stir deep wells of emotion. You can do the same, play with this idea and experiment with Muse energy in your life. See how inspiration manifests when you intentionally invite it in.

Clarissa Pinkola Estés, in Women Who Run with the Wolves, explores the creative and transformative aspects of the feminine psyche, aligning deeply with the Muse and Healer dimensions of Aphrodite. She reminds us that creativity is not only about what we produce but also about what we receive, how we allow ourselves to be moved, inspired, and changed by art, stories, and the expressions of others.

James Hillman, a key figure in archetypal psychology, speaks of the Muse's role in shaping personal mythologies. This is particularly relevant in our current transition from the Age of Pisces to the Age of Aquarius.

We are being called to rewrite our narratives, to embrace new creative expressions that have yet to emerge. This shift will heighten the Earth's vibration, allowing a reality shaped by love, imagination, and harmony to take root.

When we invite the Muse in, we invite inspiration, transformation, and the courage to create without fear. Whether through writing, painting, dance, or simply the art of living, Aphrodite's Muse archetype reminds us that we are all creators, shaping our world through passion and vision.

The Healer

Aphrodite's healing is not something external, she is the energy of activation that stems from love and already resides within us. This means that when we are activated, the alignment of the resonance between our current love vibration and that original blueprint becomes apparent. This frequency will be discussed in the next chapter, but essentially, it is the frequency of self-love, acceptance, and emotional restoration.

The cool thing about working with Aphrodite in her Healer aspect is that she has no resistance, making her energy easier to work with, it is about allowing. Emotions are energy in motion, and when we suppress them, they create blockages, but Aphrodite's energy can help us move through these energies with grace. Healing can take many forms, we can create, move our bodies, talk and explore ideas and relationships, or surrender into meditation or nature. Sometimes, the most profound healing happens when we simply allow ourselves to feel without resistance.

In therapeutic settings, the Healer archetype can be used as a tool for emotional recovery and transformation. One of my greatest works with the goddess is shadow work, something I have done for many years and many times. I actually didn't even know it was a coined term until recently, and because of this, I am sure that it is a natural part of life. If you look back, you will see that you have engaged in shadow work many times, too.

Carl Jung was the first to coin the term the shadow, referring to the unconscious aspects of the psyche that we suppress or reject. He described shadow work as the process of integrating these hidden parts of ourselves, bringing them into conscious awareness to foster wholeness. Jung believed that true individuation, the process of becoming one's most authentic self, required embracing the shadow rather than ignoring or repressing it.

Interestingly, this concept is mirrored in shamanic traditions, where soul retrieval is practiced. In indigenous healing systems, shamans believe that when we experience trauma, parts of our soul or vital energy become fragmented and lost. Through rituals, drumming, and deep meditative states, the shaman journeys into the spiritual realm to retrieve these lost soul fragments, restoring wholeness. This is very similar to Jungian shadow work, as both involve reclaiming the hidden aspects of the self to achieve healing and integration.

I love to use the story of Inanna to guide my shadow work and simply allow myself to follow the path.It is the process of integrating the hidden, wounded aspects of ourselves, essential to deep healing. To truly heal, we must be willing to look at the parts of ourselves we have exiled, the versions of us that were once too tender to hold. Aphrodite stands beside us in this process, offering her unconditional love.

Inanna's descent into the underworld is one of the oldest myths of transformation, reflecting this healing journey. She meets Ereshkigal, her shadow self, who strips her bare, forcing her to surrender all attachments. This is the essence of true healing: letting go of what no longer serves us so that we may rise anew.

The Warrior

Aphrodite's connection to war is often overlooked, but in truth, she represents the good fight. Not external conflict, but the internal battle, the struggle between resistance and surrender, between fear and love.

It is telling that mythology split Aphrodite's warrior aspect, projecting it outward into her relationship with Ares, the god of war. Yet, if we look deeper, we see that this story is actually about Aphrodite's own duality. She was once Inanna, a goddess who descended into the underworld to reclaim herself. There, she faced Ereshkigal, her darker aspect. This journey was not a battle of destruction but one of integration.

This is the war Aphrodite fights, the battle of self-remembrance. It is a war of transformation, of releasing what is no longer needed so that new growth can emerge. The Good War is not about struggle for the sake of struggle; it is about stepping into conscious evolution.

When I began writing this book, I found myself unexpectedly hospitalized for four days. It was strange, I didn't feel sick, yet my bloodwork showed a systemic infection. While recovering, I worked energetically with myself, sensing that something deeper was unfolding. I later entered meditation and found myself in the cave of Ereshkigal, processing what had happened on a level beyond the physical.

I share this story to illustrate that the Good War is always happening, whether we are aware of it or not. The key is to approach it with love, to embrace transformation rather than resist it. Aphrodite reminds us that when we fight the right battles, the ones that lead to growth and healing, we emerge reborn.

Aphrodite's light is always available. She is the Lover, the Muse, the Healer, the Warrior, and the Creator of Worlds. She flows through the elements, through the beauty of the ocean, through the shifting murmuration of birds in the sky. She is with us in every act of love, every moment of creation.

All we need to do is invite her in.

Now let's experience this goddess energy and embody the presence of Aphrodite. For this, we are going to use a meditation by the beautiful Reiki healer Rachel, who offers a potent YouTube channel filled with free Reiki sessions gifted to the world. This particular meditation was created around Beltane, but as I am in Australia, it is the opposite season here, and so I have come to understand that energy is never linear or one-sided. This meditation can help move you past that kind of thinking as well.

It is a journey into goddess energy and an activation of the goddess within. And if you don't already know, essentially all the goddesses are one goddess, it is just that, in our 3D existence, we can present them as individual faces. This can be beautiful and fun to play with, as we tap into different nuances at various stages in our lives for help, guidance, and healing. But it can also become a limitation if we do not recognize the fluidity of the faces. Goddess energy is wild and transforming all the time, that is the nature of her.

And so, this meditation offers us an experience into that living resonance. It is a gentle reminder that the Divine Feminine is not static, but a sacred dance of becoming. And a huge thank you to Rachel, blessings sister of love.

Experience the meditation here

Or look up Reiki Rachael on Youtube, @reikirachae for her Equinox Energy Activation Video in 2025. https://youtu.be/Mj7H4sutKUo?si=NkVm-XqelUKH5skC

Venus

In astrology, Venus represents love, beauty, attraction, creativity, pleasure, and self-worth. She is the planet that governs how we give and receive love, what we find beautiful, and how we experience pleasure in life. For women, Venus holds a particularly profound role, acting as a blueprint for femininity, self-expression, relationships, and the way one magnetizes abundance and connection.

Understanding your natal Venus sign is like unlocking a sacred map of your desires, values, and emotional needs. It reveals how you experience love, what makes you feel adored, and how you cultivate your own beauty and creativity. But beyond romance, Venus also guides you in self-worth, finances, and creative fulfillment, showing where you naturally attract ease and grace.

The Planet

Look at where Venus is placed in your chart in terms of elements. If any of these elements are off balance, you may feel disruptions in your life and in your connection to others. See the table below for attributes.

- Fire Venus (Aries, Leo, Sagittarius) – You are passionate, bold, and expressive. You need to receive excitement and directness from others, and you need to give yourself freedom in love.

- Earth Venus (Taurus, Virgo, Capricorn) – You are sensual, practical, and loyal. You need to receive beauty that has stability and comfort from others, and you need to gift yourself long-term security.

- Air Venus (Gemini, Libra, Aquarius) – You are intellectual, social, and playful. You need to receive valued communication and mental connection from others, and you need to gift yourself variety in your life.

- Water Venus (Cancer, Scorpio, Pisces) – You are deeply emotional and intuitive. You need to receive emotional safety and deep bonds from others, and you need to gift yourself spiritual connection.

In the House

Looking at the house placement of Venus in your natal chart reveals where you naturally attract love, abundance, pleasure, and harmony in life. Each house represents a different area of life, shaping how you express Venusian energy in relationships, creativity, and self-worth.

1. Venus in the 1st House makes a person naturally magnetic and physically attractive. People are drawn to you effortlessly, and you exude grace, charm, and harmony in a way that feels effortless. Your presence has a calming effect on others, and you likely have an innate appreciation for beauty, style, and aesthetics. However, this placement also calls for a deep journey of self-love and self-acceptance, as your outer beauty reflects the confidence you cultivate within. Learning to embrace yourself fully, inside and out, will

amplify your natural charm and radiance. Rather than seeking validation from others, developing a strong sense of self-worth will make your Venusian energy even more powerful.

2. Venus in the 2nd House enhances one's love for luxury, stability, and financial comfort. There is often a natural ability to attract wealth and material abundance, though the deeper lesson here revolves around understanding self-worth. True prosperity is not just about financial gain but about recognizing your own value. The way you allow yourself to receive love and abundance from others mirrors how you view your own worth. By cultivating gratitude and appreciating what you already have, you naturally attract more stability. Be mindful of overspending or using luxury as a way to fill emotional voids. Learning that money is an energy exchange and that you are deserving of both financial and emotional abundance will shift your perspective toward greater fulfillment.

3. Venus in the 3rd House expresses love through words, learning, and meaningful connections. Intellectual stimulation, writing, speaking, and

socializing are areas where Venus's influence is most strongly felt. You thrive in relationships that are mentally engaging, and you likely have a natural gift for communication. Expressing your love through words, whether in conversation, writing, or even through artistic expression, is vital. You may find joy in learning, traveling, and exchanging ideas with those who inspire you. However, it is important to balance mental stimulation with emotional depth. Overanalyzing emotions or relying too heavily on words to express love may sometimes limit your ability to simply feel and experience it.

4. Venus in the 4th House finds love in home, roots, and emotional security. Deep emotional bonds and a strong connection to family and ancestry are central to your sense of fulfillment. You feel happiest when your home is a sanctuary of beauty, warmth, and comfort. There is a natural inclination toward creating a harmonious domestic life, whether through nurturing relationships or cultivating a space that feels safe and inviting. If childhood wounds exist, inner healing will be essential in establishing

a stable foundation for love. Strengthening family connections, practicing forgiveness, and honoring your personal traditions can help create a sense of belonging and peace.

5. Venus in the 5th House allows love to pour through as passion, creativity, and playfulness. This is one of the most romantic placements for Venus, amplifying self-expression, artistic talent, and an appreciation for life's pleasures. You thrive in love that is joyful, grand, and filled with excitement. Creative pursuits bring deep fulfillment, as Venus here encourages artistic expression in all forms, painting, music, dance, or anything that allows you to share your unique essence with the world. Romance is often dramatic and filled with gestures of love, but it is important to stay grounded and not chase pleasure at the expense of stability. Embracing love with an open heart while also recognizing when to pause and reflect ensures long-term joy.

6. Venus in the 6th House finds love through service, health, and daily routines. There is a natural appreciation for beauty in the small, meaningful details of everyday life. You express

love through acts of service, whether by taking care of others, maintaining a harmonious routine, or tending to personal well-being. A structured approach to relationships, work, and self-care brings you happiness, but there is also a need to balance giving with receiving. If you often prioritize others' needs over your own, learning to create boundaries will help maintain inner harmony. By viewing routine as a form of devotion rather than obligation, you can cultivate a sense of pleasure in the simple, day-to-day moments.

7. Venus in the 7th House places a strong emphasis on relationships, making love and partnership a central theme in your life. This placement enhances diplomacy, grace, and a natural ability to attract meaningful connections. You thrive in committed partnerships and often seek a soulmate-like bond. Harmony, fairness, and mutual respect are key aspects of your love language. However, it is essential to cultivate self-love first so that relationships enhance your life rather than define it. Seeking external validation or depending too much on another for

emotional security can create imbalance. When you embrace your own worth, you can form deep, fulfilling partnerships that are based on equality and shared values.

8. Venus in the 8th House brings intensity, transformation, and profound emotional and physical intimacy. Love is rarely casual with this placement, it is deep, consuming, and often life-altering. Relationships act as catalysts for personal growth, uncovering hidden aspects of yourself and leading you through cycles of transformation. This placement encourages you to embrace vulnerability and trust, as opening up fully to another can be both terrifying and healing. Emotional depth is a gift, but there is also a need to release fears of betrayal or abandonment. By working through past wounds and embracing the transformative power of love, you can experience the kind of soulful connections that bring lasting fulfillment.

9. Venus in the 9th House expresses love through adventure, personal growth, and exploration. There is a deep attraction to philosophy, culture, and new experiences, and relationships

thrive on excitement and learning. You are drawn to partners who expand your perspective, whether through travel, education, or spiritual development. Love must feel liberating rather than restrictive, and you may struggle in relationships that feel stagnant or limiting. Embracing your need for independence while also forming meaningful connections will allow you to experience love in a way that aligns with your adventurous spirit. Finding ways to infuse excitement and discovery into your relationships ensures lasting fulfillment.

10. Venus in the 10th House links love, beauty, and public presence, often bringing recognition in career, social status, or personal influence. Relationships may be intertwined with professional success, and you may attract admiration for your grace and charm. There is a natural ability to create harmony in leadership roles, and your love life may be connected to your ambitions. However, it is important not to seek relationships solely for status or external validation. True fulfillment comes from aligning your career with what you genuinely love and

ensuring that personal connections are built on authenticity rather than image. By embracing your natural charisma while staying true to your heart's desires, you can find success both professionally and romantically.

11. Venus in the 11th House finds love in friendships, community, and shared visions for a better world. Social connections are deeply meaningful, and you thrive in relationships that foster mutual growth and collaboration. There is a strong appreciation for intellectual and emotional connections within groups, and love may develop from friendships or shared causes. Relationships must feel progressive, inspiring, and aligned with your higher ideals. Conventional love may not always suit you, and you may be drawn to unconventional or long-distance relationships. Embracing love in all its diverse expressions allows you to form deep, authentic connections with those who share your vision.

12. Venus in the 12th House carries a mystical, hidden, and deeply spiritual approach to love. There is a sense of longing for something beyond

the physical, and relationships may feel karmic or fated. Love may be experienced through soul connections, secret romances, or deep, unspoken emotions. This placement often brings profound compassion, but there is also a need to set healthy boundaries to avoid self-sacrifice. Finding ways to channel love through spiritual practices, creative pursuits, or acts of kindness can help bring a sense of fulfillment. True love, for you, begins within, when you learn to embrace self-love fully, you attract relationships that reflect your deepest emotional and spiritual needs.

It is good to take a look at where Venus is in both house and sign and combine this information to get a more rounded picture of what you need for love, both from yourself and what you allow yourself to receive from others. Aligning with these energies allows love and relationships to flow more easily in the vibrational aspect of life.

Conversely, if your love energy feels off, sitting with this information can help you see yourself more clearly. Like looking into a mirror, understanding your personal love story can provide a mapping effect, helping you return to yourself through alignment with these energies. Many times, astrology has given me that feeling of, "Oh, I get it now," when something was happening in my life.

It is hard to explain, but when we see ourselves reflected in our birth chart and compare that to our lived experience, we can recognize what is in harmony and what is misaligned. That gap, where we are versus where our Venus energy naturally flows, is where clarity comes in. When we acknowledge this, we gain insight into what we need to work on, allowing us to move forward with greater ease, understanding, and love.

Venus Star Points

This is a very exciting and fascinating topic for me to address in this book because I know little about it and am totally relying on research and channeling. What I do know intuitively is that the Venus star points are related to the Rose Heart Pathway. This pathway is the Priestess Pathway of Love and Trust and has been kept hidden for a long time through the esoteric teachings of Jesus and Mary Magdalene. I don't know too much more than that except that this teaching was passed to them from the high priests and priestesses of Astarte and, as mentioned previously, is documented through secret findings using the Nag Hammadi manuscripts, which is detailed in the book The Magdalene Manuscript by Tom Kenyon and Judi Sion in way more depth than I can give here.

What is even more interesting, and is occurring now, not just back then, is that these teachings are rising in the consciousness of many people. You only need to search "Rose Heart," "Mary Magdalene," and "Priestess of the Goddess" to see this knowledge reawakening through many women today. I have been doing goddess work long enough to know that this was not the case a mere 20 years ago. And yet now, much like how pyramids appeared across different civilizations at the same time, so too are these goddess mystery teachings returning.

There is a connection to higher dimensions here, and once in meditation, I went deep, deep to, well, somewhere, and there was a ray of magenta light that spoke. Or, a better way of saying it is that it telepathically transmitted information about my place in the universe. Now, I know this sounds totally weird, but it is very hard to bring back information from these states for a few reasons. One reason is that the energy is so different from the physical 3D world we know. It doesn't follow the same rules or logic, and it's not even linear. A lot of unnecessary details fall away, and you realize how irrelevant some things are. So, you can imagine how hard it is to describe these experiences when you return because the contrast is so stark.

Another reason is that you forget. While in that space, you completely understand everything instantly, it's like a memory being fully activated at once, with visuals, impressions, and deep knowing. But when I open my eyes, it's like the fine threads of what I knew start slipping away. Sometimes, I can hold on to parts of the information for longer, but eventually, it fades. This is why I'm so grateful to be writing this down now. What is a legacy if not recorded and passed on?

What we are looking at with the Venus Star Points is... cycles. Not just what you need to receive and give in love, and not just what area of life Venusian energy manifests strongest in, but how all of these things cycle over time, which is paradigm-shifting! Thank you so much to the wonderful pioneers of goddess work such as Arielle Guttman, Adam Gainsburg, and Demetra George for bringing this knowledge through.

We are all aware that we cycle, right? It's a feminine principle, and it means continuous life but also continuous transformation. The best part of knowing cycles is that we can transform with grace instead of pain. Pain only occurs when we cycle unconsciously, aka when we are forced to transform. Yep, that hurts.

Venus, up there in the cosmos, weaves through 4D space-time, forming an extraordinary celestial pentagram. How cool is it that we knew this all along? Over time, Venus' orbit creates five star points, and these points symbolize major evolutionary shifts in love, creativity, self-worth, and values. When we look at the whole story of these points through the lens of one cycle, we uncover a deeper evolutionary journey of Venus, and therefore, the story of love itself.

Venus completes her cycle in an eight-year pattern, forming a perfect five-pointed star when her conjunctions with Earth and the Sun are mapped over time. This geometric formation is unique in planetary motion and has deep symbolic significance. The pentagram has long been associated with the Divine Feminine, sacred union, and cosmic balance, studied by mystics, astrologers, and astronomers for centuries. It is a portal through which the vibrations of love, beauty, harmony, and creation enter into our Earth realm.

Each of Venus' five star points corresponds to a specific

zodiac sign, shifting every eight years. This eight-year mark represents a transition and activation of a powerful cycle, both on a personal and collective level.

Within this cycle, Venus also has five-point cycles that shift every nine months, oscillating between masculine and feminine energies.

There are:

- Small cycles (nine-month oscillations between yin & yang energy)
- Eight-year cycles (creating a five-pointed star of transformation)
- Larger, multi-generational Venus cycles (shaping collective love evolution)

The Current Venus Star Points (2020–2028)

Currently, Venus is forming Star Points in the following zodiac signs, creating an archetypal story that shapes our evolution in love, creativity, and self-worth.

January 2022 – Capricorn Star Point
This was a time of commitment, responsibility, and

building lasting value in love and finances. Many people restructured their relationships and redefined their self-worth. Personally, this was when I had my deep spiritual awakening, it restructured my relationships, my self-worth, and the way I valued life.

August 2023 – Leo Star Point
This star point focused on authentic self-expression, creative sovereignty, and love for oneself. I restarted my writing journey during this phase, fully embracing my individuality and courage to create.

June 2024 – Gemini Star Point
This star point deepened communication, curiosity, and self-expression in relationships. For me, this was when I committed fully to being a writer, confronted my fear of selling and self-worth, and embraced my role in the writing and marketing world.

March 2025 – Aries Star Point
This star point aligns with bold action, independent thinking, and initiating new desires. This is happening now, as I complete this book. I feel the energy of empowerment, taking decisive action, and stepping into leadership in my writing and career.

October 2026 – Scorpio Star Point

This upcoming star point signals deep emotional transformation, the release of old patterns, and an intense rebirth in love and intimacy. I already sense that this will align with me fully stepping into my next level as an author and business leader. Scorpio energy purges the past and initiates rebirth, which will likely coincide with a full transition into running my creative business.

Rose Heart Lineage & Venus Star Points

This ancient lineage revealed through the Venusian Star Points is something we will explore later in this book. The myth of the ages, from the perspective of the Aphrodite lineage, is known as the Rose Heart pathway, the path of love, which is intricately woven into the Venus Star Point cycles. These myths, often assumed to be purely symbolic or cultural, are actually cosmic transmissions, seeded into human consciousness from the stars themselves. The descent and rebirth of the goddess Inanna mirrors this Venus cycle, illustrating that love is not static, it must move, transform, and recycle itself for life to continue evolving. This is why the same myth, with variations, appears across different civilizations, because it carries a universal truth, transcending gender, culture, and time.

What is particularly fascinating is that while we can

intellectually trace these cosmic patterns, their true impact is felt on a much deeper level, within our relationships, our creative cycles, and the transformations we undergo. The Venus Star Point teaches us that love moves in phases, much like nature itself, guiding us through attraction, integration, separation, and rebirth. These cycles are not just personal; they are collective, shaping the evolution of love and consciousness for humanity as a whole.

One final insight to consider, in relationship astrology, when a person's natal Venus aligns with another's Venus Star Point, the connection is deeply karmic and often fated. These relationships are not always meant to last in the conventional sense, but they hold immense significance for spiritual growth, often triggering profound transformation and awakening. This idea of predestined love and evolution is something we see woven into storytelling as well. As I write this, I am reading Dark Fae by Caroline Peckham and Susanne Valenti, and even though it is a fantasy novel, it conveys the same core truth, love as a force of destiny, alchemy, and soul evolution. This is how magic works, through patterns, cycles, and synchronicities that remind us we are always in dialogue with the cosmos.

Symbols

Symbols are the language of the soul. They can be used, crafted, played with, or meditated upon, offering whispers of unseen vibrations into awareness and creation. Symbols act as doorways, portals through which wisdom moves, crossing time, memory, and the very fabric of existence. The goddess has always spoken through symbols, leaving them like breadcrumbs along the path of remembrance, waiting for those ready to see.

The moon and her cycles serve as a perfect representation of a goddess symbol. Multilayered, multidimensional, she holds many meanings at once, yet always carries the key of truth. Below is a list of Aphrodite's symbols, each holding a unique resonance, a key to the deeper mysteries of love.

This part of the path is yours alone, as it has always been and always will be. Through love and trust, these living energies can be worked with, embodied, and understood. In your own way, they will guide you home to the essence of love itself.

Pentagram - There is a rhythm to love, a pulse that beats beneath all things. It is the hum of creation, the breath of the universe, the dance of life itself. It does not ask, nor does it demand, it simply is, waiting for those who remember to align with its eternal song. The Pentagram of Love is not a shape to be drawn but a living portal of energy, a celestial pattern traced by the steps of Venus in the heavens, whispering secrets into the hearts of those who dare to listen. Five points, five keys, five initiations, each a doorway, each a remembering. Beneath its shape, beneath its pattern, lives the deeper truth: Love is never stagnant. It moves, it cycles, it renews. Like the ever-turning spiral of the rose, the deep pull of the ocean tide, the unfurling of wings into flight, love transforms. It is the descent and the ascent, the journey of the goddess through time, through shadow, through surrender, and through rebirth. The symbols are already known to you, written into your bones, woven through your soul's story. They do not need to be learned, only remembered.

Huluppu Tree - Long ago, Inanna found the tree. A sacred gift carried by the waters, its roots reaching into the dark soil, its branches stretching toward the heavens. It was a bridge, as all trees are, a place of gathering, a place of transformation. The Huluppu Tree, they say, stood at the edge of the world, where the known and the unknown meet. The place in between. The same space that Asherah once occupied, her sacred tree standing as a living pillar of the cosmos, a reminder that life and love are both rooted and untamed. The tree is the mother. She is Ninhursag, holding the first forms of life in her embrace. She is wisdom, she is shelter, she is the knowing that endures even when all else falls away. Her roots hold the stories of those who came before; her branches carry the dreams of those who will come after. To stand beneath her is to stand at the crossroads. There is a whisper in the leaves, a call from the ancestors: "Come," they say, "sit at our feet, press your hands to the earth. Feel the wisdom beneath your skin, the stories in your blood. The tree does not ask you to stay, only to know. And when you are ready, to rise." The pentagram begins with the tree, with the knowing that love is both deep and vast, a rooted thing, a reaching thing. It does not belong to us, but we belong to it.

Doves - She circles above, white wings catching the light, casting shadows upon the temple stone. She is the messenger, the carrier, the presence of peace. Aphrodite knew the language of doves, as did Inanna before her. The silent beat of their wings spoke of prayers lifted, of burdens released. In temples long forgotten, the air was filled with their soft coos, their presence marking spaces where the veil between the seen and unseen had thinned. They tell us to listen, not with our ears, but with our hearts. To release what is heavy, to trust the wind to carry it where it needs to go. When the world grew hard, when love was bound and sacrificed, they said the doves were taken too. But listen, can you hear them? They still fly. They still carry the breath of the goddess, whispering the language of love into the bones of those who remember. The second point of the pentagram is the breath, the movement, the release. Love is not meant to be held captive. It must be allowed to fly.

Rose - The rose does not bloom all at once. It unfolds, petal by petal, layer by layer, revealing itself to the world. Not in haste, but in rhythm. It knows its time, it trusts the cycle. The rose is the path of love, the journey inward, the unfurling of the heart. It is sacred geometry, the fingerprint of Venus, the language of the priestesses who came before us. It is the softness of the beloved, the sharpness of the thorn. It is beauty, but it is also protection. Inanna carried the scent of the rose when she descended into the underworld. Astarte wore it upon her brow, a crown of both power and surrender. Aphrodite, the weaver of love, left them in her wake. They were not tokens, but symbols of what must be learned. Love is not given, it is grown, cultivated, tended to, and honored. It is the patience of a thousand petals opening, the willingness to let go of what has already withered. The third point of the pentagram is the rose, the unfolding, the trust in divine timing.

Ocean - In the place where the waves kiss the shore, something ancient stirs. Aphrodite rose from the sea, they say. Born from the foam, carried by the tide, stepping onto the earth as love incarnate. But before her, the ocean was already singing. Hold the shell to your ear. What do you hear? It is the sound of the beginning, the first breath, the first word, the first knowing that love has always existed. The shell carries it, an echo of the great womb of creation, a reminder that we are born from the sea, from the stars, from the great, endless current of love itself. This is the fourth point of the pentagram: the remembering. That love is ancient, that love is eternal, that love is the current that carries us home.

One by one, the points are drawn. Rooted in the tree, carried by the dove, unfolding through the rose, whispered in the seafoam's song. The last point, the final mark, is neither seen nor touched. It is the space between, the luminous thread that binds them all. It is the breath between words, the stillness between heartbeats. It is the knowing, the trust, the surrender to the great mystery. The priestesses knew. They traced the pentagram in the sand, in the stars, in the movements of their own lives. It was never a symbol to be worn, but a map to be walked, a path not just of love, but of creation itself. Love does not stay still. It does not stagnate. It moves, it shapes, it becomes. This is what the Venus Star Points have always been telling us, that is a living force, a sacred rhythm, a cosmic spell woven into all things.

And now, it is yours. Step into the pattern. Follow the path. Remember what you have always known. Love is not something we seek. It is something we are. The Pentagram of Love is drawn. The portal is open. It is up to you to walk.

Rituals

Rituals are essentially points in our day where we consciously connect with the day. The awesome thing, that took me a long time to really get, is that they don't have to be elaborate but can be in every moment, all the time. The more you practice rituals, the more you will do them, and the more your existence will be divine and divinely led.

And yes, the big ones are awesome and have a power of their own, but we also want to live a magical life, not just do magic from time to time. To embody and make real, we just need to experience it and practice and grow the experience into our own version of living aligned with the divine essence of being. I am fairly sure that is what Jesus and Mary Magdalene did, and that is the rose heart path they forged, that of being awake to the beauty of life all the time.

The word mindfulness comes to mind when I think about it. When I have clear and aligned moments of ritual in my everyday, I feel present in that moment, mindful without mind but in totality of what is happening around me and within me, and I also feel connected to the larger picture. This is also known as yoga, as yoga is not just stretching and body movements but a way of living that unites us to everything.

So we are very blessed to be able to enter, feel, and embody this experience of the divine whenever we want; we just have to remember. Remember that it is already there, we have just added too much to it to sometimes see. And it is through practicing sacred moments in our every day, practicing meditations and thinking-clearing techniques, healing ourselves, being in nature, and calling on goddess energy that we remember.

Each one of the rituals below is a flowing movement, just like the energy of Aphrodite, just like love itself, so allow it to be your version, and maybe each time it will be different. That is OK, we want to get away from structure, as it is one of the things that pushes us to forget. The sacred is already there, always present, waiting. The only question is, are you present with it?

Aphrodite's essence is sensuality, and so we will use the opening of our senses to embrace the beauty of the now. Surrender into the experience, let go of the control of your thoughts and expectations to uncover what is truly there. Step into deep embodiment by letting go, where every breath, every touch, every sensation becomes a portal to remember who you truly are. These are rituals of offering your smaller self to your higher self, your patterning of the thinking mind to the remembrance. There is nothing to force, only a presence to surrender into.

The rituals are open and non-descriptive on purpose. My intention is to trigger you to practise and develop your own connection to goddess, every day, so they are a doorway and a soft guide to help you practise.

The Ritual of Water: A Sacred Bath, A Sea Soak, A Love Offering

Water is the first womb, the first memory. Water holds

the echoes of all that has ever been, and the ability to wash away what no longer serves, offering renewal with every touch. Entering into water or having water enter into you with intention holds sacred magic and is a returning, to yourself, to the flow of life, to the place where love is not something given but something that has always been.

Perhaps it is a bath, warm and scented with rose petals, salt, and oil, a love offering, a ritual of softness. Perhaps it is the sea, the salt air brushing your skin, the waves rolling in like breath, a magic pulsing with rhythm and older than human time. Or perhaps it is a shower before you go to work or a cold drink of water on a hot day. All of these moments in time are portals to ritual and sacred union.

Before you step into the bath or ocean, connect with your higher self. All you need to do is feel it. Whisper your name to the water, feel the water and remember water as an old friend. Your body is made up of mostly water, and you can connect with the water in your body to the water without.

If you are immersed in the water, let it hold you, caress you and remember you. All of these moments with water are little miracles, like a child being held by the mother. Immerse yourself in the sensation of it, feel it, call Aphrodite as she is the goddess who was born from water.

You can commune with her too. When you finish, let the droplets slip from your skin like a final blessing, feel the water run down your throat knowing it will always be with you and also circulate through the whole earth's water cycles. You are a part of everything. Everything comes back to you in the form of water and is a part of you.

The Ritual of Air: Listening to the Birds, the Song of the Wind

The wind does not need words to speak. It carries stories older than memory, ones that are only intuited and are activating. In my book Awakening Lilith, we uncover a hidden truth that Lilith, before being put into words and story form, was the wind. And so we can see the connection between her and Aphrodite here in the sensual experience of the wind in ritual.

Do you remember what it is like to feel the voices of the wind that hum through leaves? What about the sounds that enter your ear and give you pause, yet have been crafted by the waves? Can you go outside and allow the hush of a morning sunrise to wash over your senses and connect you to the divine?

These are the rituals that connect the essence of Aphrodite to our senses and our earth. How wonderful that we are alive to partake in the everyday blessings. How joyous are we to know this and have this available to us wherever we are in the world and whatever circumstances we find ourselves in.

If you have ever stood beneath trees at midday, listening, truly listening, you have felt it, the language beyond language. The ritual of love beyond ritual. Step outside when the world is quiet, and if you can't step, ask someone to assist you. Feel the air against your skin, the unseen touch of something vast and eternal. Listen to the rustle of leaves, allow the sweet bird call to teach you something new.

The hush between sounds is also there, like a breath in. It calls to transformation and mystery. There is deep magic there, so let yourself be unheard within it. Let yourself be received. A breath in, slow. A breath out, softer. Walk away lighter. This pause is ritual, it is where we walk between worlds. Something has been given and something has been received.

The Ritual of Resonance: AUM, the Sacred Resonance of Creation

Everything that exists moves in rhythm. We feel this fundamental movement as vibrations, and the vibrations have the ability to form connections. These connections have their own experience and agenda, and rules are set upon them for different experiences to occur in realities. One of these experiences is what we call life in human incarnate. But it is possible to know this essence through practice, and the benefit we get from such practice is a stripping away of debris. The practices are like a key opening a doorway that brings in fresh air and expandedness that offers freedom and increased unconditional love and peace.

One of my teachers in this life, and perhaps others, is Sadhguru, who helped me understand what the vibrations I was feeling during my spiritual awakening were. For about a year and a half, I had no idea what was happening, but I quickly settled into enjoying the experience. I often took myself to bed early just to lay in vibration. Although I am still learning the language of vibration, I have learned that there are different types, well, they feel different, and that we can ask for and channel vibrations through our bodies for healing, love, the processing of pain and grief, or simply for pure bliss.

Sadhguru explains that everything moves, our body, our breath, even the stars spinning in the vastness of space. Movement and vibration are also known as sound, which is why some people resonate so strongly with it. Sound is not just heard; it is felt and carried through bone, blood, and spirit. This pleasure connects us to our authentic self, and that touchpoint from one paradigm to the next is miraculous.

This ritual is a ritual of calling sound vibrations through your body, to align, to vibrate with the same pulse of the cosmos, AKA your higher self.

To do this, we are using three sounds, which essentially

form one sound. We change the shape of our mouth from fully open to mid-open to closed in order for the sound to vibrate differently inside our bodies. The sound we say is 'A,' and as we close our mouth, it naturally changes to 'U' and then to 'M.' Each of these different vibrations also resonates in different parts of the body, and I like to think of this as the kundalini rising, starting in your belly with 'A,' moving up through your heart and throat with 'U,' and then to your third eye with 'M.'

It is important to note that you don't have to make deliberate mouth movements. Simply closing your mouth slowly changes the vibration naturally. If you would like to learn this directly from the master, I highly recommend checking the resources section to connect with the Isha Foundation and learn the original technique yourself.

AUM Breaths

A breath in, deep and full. Ahhh, Ooooh, Mmmm.

Feel it in your chest, your throat, your skull.

Beyond your body, beyond time.
Again, the breath. Again, the sound.

Sadhguru's teachings speak of AUM as a portal that reflects the primordial vibration of existence itself. It is the sound of creation, preservation, and dissolution. When sounding this, the body becomes a temple, the sound becomes a bridge, and your awareness begins to dissolve into the field of intelligence that sustains all life.

In yogic science, this alignment is called Nada Yoga, the yoga of sound, and it is known to cleanse karma, balance the energy body, and awaken deeper perception. It's the vibration of the spine straightening, the energy rising, the subtle body remembering itself. He explains that the syllables of AUM represent the three fundamental dimensions of the human system:

"A" vibrates in the lower body, activating the base, your connection to the Earth and physicality.
"U" moves through the chest and heart, awakening emotions, breath, and the space of connection.
"M" travels into the head and beyond, touching the mind, intuition, and the infinite.

Even the non-physical realms, the energies beyond the five senses, respond to this sound. Chanting AUM refines your body system, harmonizes your chakras, and expands your receptivity. You don't need to "understand" it. It is the experience that brings the understanding, not the other way around. The resonance does the work. The sound carries intelligence. You are simply the vessel that receives and transmits it.

The Ritual of Reflection: Mirror Work & Self-Love

The mirror does not lie. It does not flatter, nor does it condemn. It simply reflects, offering back to you the image of who you are in this moment, without judgment and without distortion. And yet, so often, we avoid it. We turn away. We see only the flaws, the imperfections, the stories we've been told about what beauty should be.

It's interesting that the mirror is an ancient technique for scrying. It acts as a portal between our 3D world and higher realms, and the reflections that return to us are expressions of our own vibrations in the moment, particularly as they relate to our questions.

So, we can work with mirrors in two powerful ways: one, by using them to affirm our inner beliefs through spoken affirmations and acknowledgments; and two, by looking beyond the veil to uncover hidden truths. We'll call the first practice mirror manifesting, and the second scrying.

I only recently learned scrying at a witches' weekend last year. It was wonderful. Although a little harder than crystal ball work, I found that you just need more time and stillness to access the message. Truthfully, all the messages come from within you anyway, the mirror simply helps draw them out and reflect them back. It's the practice of being with yourself and observing that you're truly doing.

If you're going to scry, use a dedicated mirror, one that you clean regularly, wrap in cloth, and keep just for this purpose. When you're ready to ask a question, write it down on a piece of paper. Then, clear the space around you using whatever method feels most aligned. I work mostly with energy and intuition, so I'll often wave my hands, move the energy, and speak words to make the space sacred and honor my feelings.

Sometimes I call in protection if I'm feeling vulnerable, and other times, if I'm fully embodied in presence, those fears simply don't exist.

Once the space is ready, open your mirror and allow your

gaze to soften. Let your spirit open to the greater You. Ask your question, then jot down what you see or sense. Don't worry about making sense of it right away, we want to bypass the thinking mind and its limitations. When you feel complete, offer gratitude, cleanse the space, and wrap your mirror up with care.

While still in sacred space, review what you wrote down. Keep your thinking mind soft and open. Let insights arise as you reread. Often, the answer will reveal itself in that moment, almost like it slips between the lines. Write it down. It may be subtle, like a thin, etheric thread that disappears once the energy shifts. When you're ready, close the space however you like. Even a small smile and a connection to gratitude is enough to deepen the resonance of spiritual connection in your everyday life. This simple presence is an important step in embodying the love of a divinely led life.

Aphrodite sees beauty not only in the inner realms, but also in the material world. And so, standing before the mirror becomes an act of devotion, to her, and to yourself. It is a remembering and a reclamation of your own self-love.

You can use any mirror for this. Simply look into your

own eyes. Hold your gaze. A remembering will come. Tell yourself that you love yourself, even when it feels uncomfortable, even when the voice of doubt rises up. Whisper: “I see you. I honor you. I love you.”

Build this into your life. Don’t just speak the words, feel them. Let the vibration of love flow through your body. Let it become real. Because it is.

Fogotten

When this book first began calling to me, channeling itself through my awareness, I mistook the signs I was receiving about Aphrodite for another goddess, the goddess Oshun. The two goddesses have similarities in terms of their connection to water, sensuality and fertility, and in that moment, as I was floating over big rolling waves in a green-blue sea that filled my heart with joy and bliss, the ocean sang to me. As so this journey began.

Later that day when I thought of Oshun, I kept getting a "no, not quite right" feeling, and as the days rolled on, and more magical moments happened I realized that Oshun was a Goddess known for riverways and not oceans and so I contemplated other goddesses. This is how it always starts with these goddess books, magical, divine moments which I feel and am so blessed to experience. Before the linear thinking mind kicks I get to be in just the energy of the archetype. Eventually, not being sure which goddess I was with, I just asked "Which goddess is calling and speaking with me?" and I drew out the Aphrodite card from my Goddess Oracle.

At that moment, I was hit with certainty, and then I was like, "no, that can't be right," as I usually work with the more underworld and deep archetypes. At least, that's what I thought, until now, at the time of finishing this book, I realized that no, I have always worked with both sides. I could only see the more unusual ones because they were more obvious and stood out from 'normal', but the softer, more loving ones were always there in my life. It's funny what you don't even see about yourself sometimes, that which is obvious to others. The faces of Goddess are never separate anyways and that is why I love goddess work, because it unveils truths of me to me. It does not attempt to tell me who I should be, it only provides a pathway to a lived experience of unfolding of who I am.

Anyway, I remember spending that afternoon on my bed going through all the goddess oracle cards and intuitively pulling out all the ones that sent that impulse of vibrational match to my current inclinations. I played with the cards I pulled for a while, put them into different piles, removed some, and this was all done in a playful, explorational kind of way, without too much thinking and more an intuitive lightness and fascination. Eventually, I was left with a few cards and I placed them on my altar, which is also my bedside table (I'm practical, if anything). When I woke the next morning, I knew it was Aphrodite calling me, it kind of sweeped into the in between realms of conscious and unconscious as I fell asleep and woke again. I was completely certain, and that was that.

I started writing the book as I always do, having absolutely no idea what I was going to write and, boom, my fingers were like magical wands creating real magical ideas right before my eyes. Time passed, and as I immersed myself deeper into the work, I realized that Aphrodite was revealing herself to me in many layers that I didn't even know she had. I think that's why I resisted her initially, because I just assumed her depth was only in the 3D and on the physical material plane. I didn't see myself as that type of person (although I could appreciate it in others and in the world), and through that naivety and that self-made disconnection, I created some sort of barrier. Luckily, she persisted, and I am so glad to have reclaimed that part of myself, which now has made me fall in love with the material world in a uniquely different way, an unexpected way, but one very beautiful and full of sacred promise.

Two months into my research, I was led back through my ideas and writing to a full-circle moment, back to where I started, and the goddess Oshun, the Yoruba goddess of rivers, fertility, and love. This spiral dance we go on when we do goddess work is quite literally magic. It doesn't move in straight lines, but in waves and rhythms, returning us to places we thought we had already understood, only to show us new depths. In that return, I began to see, through Aphrodite's eyes, all her connections to previous incarnations, archetypes, and stories from other cultures and lineages. It was as if the veils between them lifted, revealing an ancient thread woven through time. That's when I felt called to go back and include the timeline into the book, not just as historical fact, but as energetic remembrance. Of course, linear time is not just backward but also forward, and the spiral continues to expand. The future is luminous with the reemergence of the Rose Heart pathways, codes of love, devotion, and divine remembrance, opening again in collective consciousness. I'll speak more about that in the next chapter. But even now, if you look out into the world with clear eyes and an open heart, you'll see it: Rose Heart mystery schools, sacred sisterhoods, and priestess temples rising again. It is a very exciting time for the goddess. She is not returning, she has always been here and it is women that are the ones remembering. What was once forgotten can be reawakened.

She is the goddess who dares to love through every phase, not just the blissful ones. She holds you when you are weeping on the floor, when you are lost, when you are longing for something unnamed. She is not just the kiss on your lips or the joy of sunlight on your skin, she is the ache that precedes the joy, the longing that leads you home. Her temple is not just found in sacred rituals but in the daily dance of being human. In the mess, in the mundane, in the heartbreaks and healing, she whispers, This too is sacred.

When we walk this path, the invitation is not to become more of something you are not, it is to become more of who you already are. Each moment of honesty, each breath of presence, each time you choose tenderness instead of defence, is a devotional act. That is goddess work. That is remembering. And from that remembrance, love is no longer an act we try to do, it becomes a state we live from.

What I'm beginning to understand is that Aphrodite's face is not fixed. She shows up differently for each of us. For some, she is the lover who awakens desire. For others, she is the healer who guides the release of old pain. For some, she is the warrior demanding truth. And for others still, she is the artist, the muse, the sacred rebel breaking every rule to live in beauty. She will not be pinned down. And perhaps that is her greatest teaching, that love itself is the most fluid, expansive, unknowable force we can ever touch. It cannot be tamed, only met.

So don't look for her only in the rose petals and soft skin. Look for her in the fire of your becoming. In the choices you make when no one is watching. In the voice that says yes to your soul and no to the patterns that keep you small. She is in the moment you forgive yourself. She is in the tears you finally let fall. She is in the breath you take when you choose to live fully, despite it all.

In this book, Aphrodite was my catalyst to see myself, an aspect that I had hidden from myself about beauty, pleasure, and softness. This catalyst has provoked a potential paradigm shift within me which has yet to fully unfold, but I can feel it in my solar plexus. I will dance the spiral dance without friction, as I have now remembered I can call on Aphrodite when I am in need of softness in transformation, or in need of pleasure during the tougher times of life.

I know you are here because you understand this deeper hidden truth that Aphrodite has gifted me: that which is forgotten can be remembered, not through words but through your own experience. She can be your catalyst to change everything, if you want. And it can be done in a way that is not destructive, but graceful. This is where we find the hidden face of Aphrodite, the one lost from common memory.

The other side of the coin doesn't have to be what we have been taught is the opposite. We have the power to change that through our memory, by having goddess experiences. The opposite of light is not dark, it is the absence of light, which is the void and the eternal womb where everything is lovingly created and emerges.

The opposite of peace is not war, it is transformation. And if we remember, we can do it gracefully and in the highest vibrations for the best of all. The opposite of good is not evil, it is nothing, as good is an act that creates a feeling. And so, you see, we just have to remember what is forgotten and ditch the old tired retellings of what is. We have the power to do that.

So Aphrodite is not only the goddess of love but all of matter, which is vibrationally linked to waters. Water is not just water but a structural container of information, which is more fuel than most structures. Water creates entire worlds within itself and forges itself into being. How marvelous it is that within a single body of water, an entire ecosystem exists, sustaining life in harmony, each part reaffirming and protecting the whole. It is good to think of Aphrodite in this way, not as an image of beauty confined to the surface, shaped by the fleeting ideals of a single culture or era, but as something deeper, something essential and life-sustaining. Beauty is not just an aesthetic; it is the word we use to describe the miracle of existence itself.

Now you can see why a goddess who holds this power could never have been pushed away by the patriarchy or from consciousness. The real shift was not her removal from the world, but from our memory, a forgetting imposed by systems that told us what to think, rather than encouraging a lived expression of life that remembers itself.

The love of life itself, as opposed to the love of a single fleeting form, is her true gift. There is the expansive, universal love, the love that exists in all things, flowing through creation like an eternal current. And then there is the love that is small and personal, shaped by individual perception, influenced by time, culture, and experience. Aphrodite reminds us that both exist, but one is infinite, while the other is only a perspective.

Aphrodite's message, much like Oshun's, is that love is not about holding on, it is about allowing. To love is to surrender to the current, to trust that even when waters are turbulent, they are leading you somewhere new. The goddess of love does not promise stillness; she promises transformation.

This is where we stand now, at the precipice of understanding. And this understanding is my High Priestess work in this lifetime. What is yours?

Aphrodite's war is not about destruction, it is about courage. The courage to face ourselves and remember. The courage to let go and surrender into that memory, as it is already there, just buried under all the thought forms of what we have been told. The courage to surrender to transformation. This is the path of the goddess, and it is the path we all must walk if we wish to truly know love.

The modern world has forgotten this deeper aspect of Aphrodite. She has been reduced to an image, a goddess of beauty, vanity, and shallow desire. But she is so much more than that. She is the force that calls us to love fiercely, to create without fear, to embrace change rather than resist it. She is the alchemical fire that forges us into who we are meant to be.

It is time to remember her in her fullness. To honor not just the soft and gentle Aphrodite, but the warrior. The goddess of transformation. The one who reminds us that love, above all else, is the most powerful force in the universe, not because it is soft, but because it is unstoppable.

So I ask again, what is your High Priestess work in this lifetime? What battle are you fighting within yourself? And are you ready to surrender to the transformation that awaits?

Channeling

To love yourself is not indulgence, that has been a hard pill for me to energetically swallow. I know it mentally, it's like duh of course, but energetically, there is work to be done. It has been a lifelong process to learn that devotion is the gift we offer ourselves, a sacred honoring of our unique path. The steps we take on the path dissolve the noose around our neck, those constrictions we've inherited or created, allow us to love more freely and create more beautifully. Just this morning, I was in a healing meditation about being OK with doing nothing, but rather simply allowing life to wash over and integration to occur during all the busyness that seems to be on the rise. This, too, is devotion.

My journey has led me to become an oracle and channeler of goddess energy. I'm actually pretty normal in my appearance, simple in my rituals, and practical in my everyday approach, but energetically, I am merged with my greater self. This merging wasn't taught to me through books, it was shaped through the lived experiences of my life.

When I was young, I used to pray that I would be safe and strong and beautiful, inside and out. Now that I'm in my 40s, I feel I am all those things and more. I don't usually pray for much, but sometimes I do, especially when I sense a block on my path. Mostly, I sit with gratitude. I feel and allow the spiritual energy to run through my being and ground down into the earth. It's not always dramatic, but sometimes it is, mostly it is just deeply present in the moment.

When I first started writing this series, Awakening the Goddess Within, I didn't know I could channel. The signs had been there since my spiritual awakening in 2020, but because it happened through my personal experience, not through a teacher or course, I had to come to that realization slowly over time. Now it is very clear to me that this is my path. I am a High Priestess, a name that, to me, simply means "she who works directly with goddess energy and shares that energy back out to the community."

Aphrodite has softened the claiming of the title, because that is her wonderfly energy, it is simply just true in my existence and from my perspective. She does worry herself to make others comfortable because she knows her beauty. She does not wait for permission to be radiant because it just is. She loves as the ocean loves the shore, without hesitation, without apology, without condition. And she asks you to do the same, no she tells you to choose to do the same.

Channeling has become a part of my life, and I kind of don't really think too much about it, it's just a lived experience. What I know of the channeling experience mostly stems from sitting down to write, as the words just pour through my being and my fingers are like magical wands typing words and meaning into existence that I moistly didn't know before, useless it is from my history. Apart from that, I also receive knowledge in deep meditations, but it is a little different, as it is less flowing and more like a full download, a complete understanding of an answer to a question I never asked. But when it comes, it's also like I get the question and the reason why this knowledge is available now all in one.

I also get visuals too in deep meditation. Mostly colours, kind of like vibrant light colours on a vast, spacious black background. Sometimes the 'colours' have a full meaning and story to them that comes through. And often what happens is new information, I've never heard of before, but over the next six months, it comes to me in reality. It feels like synchronicity when this happens, and it sometimes blows me away and also makes me laugh in acknowledgement.

I don't really know what others think channeling is, but I do know that it feels magical and made of unconditional love. It connects me to the universe and to a picture of myself that is bigger than just me in this incarnation. In a way, you could say it is like taking a breath, like the feeling of breathing being a sacred kiss between your inner being and your much larger, higher self.

The dance between the inner and outer worlds is mystical, because there is something about it that reveals a hidden depth. Who is it that is doing this? Is it you? Is it Goddess? These are the big questions, ones that will never be answered in words. Because it's not about who, it is about realizing the dance itself is happening, and that you are within it. To breathe with awareness like this is to participate in the eternal mystery of life. To be mindful of receiving and giving, and to acknowledge that there is something in between the two, something that transforms one into the other in our experience.

This type of breathing is exactly like the experience of channeling. You are not doing anything, but you are conscious of the flow between one to the other, and the allowing of transformation of the flow. You are the witness of this part of yourself, and over time, you can draw that into being in some way. Whether it's just for you to have magic in your life, or perhaps to share stories of connection to the Great Spirit around the campfire, or to create a painting that someone buys for their home that helps them resonate with the universe.

It is quite hard to put the experience into words, and only through sitting with yourself, in both your higher and lower forms, can it be brought into the 3D. But if you want the experience, then meditation is a great and safe way to move into connection, and I mean real connection, with the divine. I know sitting shows you your mind is busy. That happens to me too. But when someone says to me, "I can't meditate because my mind is too busy," they are literally saying the exact reason why they should meditate, as a reason not to meditate. It's the same as saying, "I'm so thirsty, but I can't drink anything because

I don’t like it.”

When your mind settles, you will know, as a powerful doorway into your higher self opens, and it’s as obvious as the difference between being asleep and awake. In the beginning, the doorway may just open for a moment, but over time it will be easier to call the door and walk through. Eventually, the door will never shut and even just disappear altogether. Once this happens you will see that it was never there in the first place. You just constructed it with the power of your thoughts and that busy mind you wanted to avoid at the beginning when you didn't want to sit and meditate. And when this happens, you will know the whole universe. Magic will be a part of your life, your breath will caress your inner and outer experience that will and you will be aware of it. This is the path of the goddess: to open this door, to walk through, and to let it dissolve into the void, and for you to stand in your power and choose what is next.

Aphrodite walked this path. She arose from the sea, from the emotional depths, fully formed. She came out of her memory and looked upon a new world and chose to bring beauty into being. She drew up the energy of her past experiences and transformed them into love light, paving the way, creating pathways of connection in the in-between, where that love light energy could flow into her creations.

We can also look at this in an as above, so below way. She descended into the earth realm from the heavens, through the stars. Her light blazes down through the Venus star story and is part of a greater cyclic journey along the rose heart pathways. This information is still new to me, and so I can only offer you this, her path is a path into merging with her other parts. This rose, formed in the star-filled universe, is an offering of love to humanity. The rose light codes descending into the human experience are profound, of a 5D nature, and must be learned through experience, not the thinking mind.

This mirrors her rising from the emotional depths to create union, but here, it is a descent from the stars to embody more love light frequency for human evolution. So you can see we are that in-between being lit up. What would you create, or not create, if you took this power in?

I am creating more love in the world. My love is not so much physical beauty, but the beauty of work and energy, and it is being birthed through you by reading this book. If this is true for you then know that I didn't do this activation, you did. You called forth this information in a union between our energies, mine, Aphrodite's, and other Goddesses. Other people have participated in this calling too, and this is the challenge from another perspective. To see, you already have this power within.

As we move into the Aquarian Age, time and space become more palpable, because this is part of human awakening and our evolution. I don't know where it will go, because we are talking about a multiverse, multi-timelines, and magic is a word that captures this with ease. It is a true pleasure to be magical and lead a magical life, something I used to pray for when I was little. And oh, how wonderful that it is now being real in my world and now channeling has come into my consciousness and this further connects me to the Divine Feminine in all her forms.

Sometimes it's Aphrodite speaking through the way my body craves beauty and rest. Other times, it's Lilith, fierce and raw, pushing me to speak a truth I've been swallowing. Isis often arrives in ritual, through dreams or symbols. I don't channel just one voice, I am open to the archetypal wisdom that lives in the collective feminine consciousness. It moves through me in the language of myth, image, feeling, and poetry. It becomes more than just archetypal and sales further through the veil. You do not have to be a mystic or a priestess to access this. It is your birthright. You don't need to wait for permission or initiation. You simply have to choose to listen.

From an esoteric standpoint, channeling is the act of becoming a clear vessel. The clearer your energy, the more easily the spirit can move through you. This is why presence, breath, stillness, and heart-opening practices are essential. The channel is not "somewhere else", it is your own body, your own awareness, aligned and receptive. When we release mental clutter, soften into the heart, and stay grounded, we open a doorway. Spirit, higher self, goddess energies, whatever you call it, meet us there.

Sadhguru says that the most profound intelligence is not found in thinking, but in stillness. He teaches that true perception comes when we stop filtering reality through our memory and conditioning. Channeling, in his view, is not about "receiving from outside," but about becoming so inwardly expansive that you tap into the source of creation itself. This is the ultimate channel: not accessing something other, but remembering that you are it.

Every time you breathe, you have a chance to remember. With each inhale, you can squeeze your pelvic floor and inner core, feeling the gentle pressure shift the kundalini energy upward into your third eye. And as you exhale, you can surrender, allowing your breath to carry what has been altered and alchemized, giving it back to the world. You are a vessel of love, always receiving, always giving.

Three breaths like this, while basking in Aphrodite's pink light, are enough to train your body to recognize receiving as a gift.

If desires arise, becoming aware of why we desire something doesn't necessarily change the desire itself, but it changes everything around it. It allows us to see the hidden threads that weave through our longings, the deeper truths beneath the surface.

When you live with the practice of consciously receiving love and giving love back into the world, patterns emerge. The interconnectedness of all things becomes visible. Karma itself, energy set into motion by our past actions, becomes clearer. And in this clarity, we begin to untangle the deeper lessons embedded within our desires.

Desire is not just about wanting, it is the force that shapes the world. Every action we take in pursuit of what we long for creates energy. It sets things in motion (karma). And if we can see these patterns, we gain the power to refine them, to align them with the highest expression of ourselves.

This chapter on channeling begins with an essential truth: creativity is a sacred current. And sometimes, when we are truly open, that current begins to speak. That is how this book began, not from a structured outline or a carefully planned concept, but from a whisper. A pulse of knowing. The sense that something, or some energy, was asking to come through. I didn't know then what channeling was. I only knew that I was writing words that felt like they were arriving from somewhere else, and yet, from within.

As I continued, I realized I was not simply creating, I was remembering. Remembering how to listen to the unseen. Remembering how to make space within myself so that something greater could move through me. This is channeling to me, a surrender of ego, a softening of the mental grip, and a trust in the unseen. It is not about becoming someone else, but about letting go enough to become more fully yourself.

Channeling doesn't always arrive in grand, cosmic waves. Sometimes, it is a single line whispered in the quiet.

Sometimes, it is a feeling that floods your body, a knowing that settles deep in your bones. It comes through words, yes, but also through images, sensations, and impulses that feel like home. Like the truth.

To channel is to collaborate with spirit. With Goddess and your own soul. And the clearer you become, the more you tend to your inner world, your body, your energy, the easier it becomes to hear. The goddess speaks in many ways, through archetype, through nature, through the subtle nudges you feel when something is right, even if it makes no sense at all.

What began for me as a way to express myself has become a living, breathing spiritual practice. I channel through writing, through ritual, through the breath, and through presence. And every time I sit to write, I begin with the same invocation that calls the goddess in, I open myself to truth. I open myself to the highest good. I allow myself to be a vessel.

Channeling is not about perfection. It is about presence. It is not about getting it "right," but about being willing to receive what wants to come through you. The more you trust yourself, the clearer the channel becomes. The more you love yourself, the more love can move through you.

Channeling, for me, is not something I "do" in a ceremonial sense, it is my life, my way of being. It is the thread that weaves my intuition, my happy place, my creativity, my emotions, and my soul into one coherent flow. Channeling shows up in my life in the quietest of ways, when I'm walking in nature and I suddenly hear a phrase drop into my awareness like a whisper from beyond. It appears when I sit down to write and entire passages pour out faster than my conscious mind can keep up.

It's not that I disappear during channeling, it's that I become more me than ever before. A clearer, truer version of myself emerges, held by something greater. In daily life, channeling informs my choices, not loudly, not telling me what to do, it's a deep resonance in the body, a knowing in my gut or a soft pull in my chest that says, this is the way. I don't make decisions from fear or logic alone anymore. I listen inward. I wait for alignment. I play energetically and when I feel that quiet click of truth, I know it's time to act.

That guidance doesn't always look "spiritual" from the outside. It might lead me to make a business shift, catalayse a change in relationship dynamic, or cancel a plan. But every one of those actions is sacred, because it comes from Source.

Lineage

There is a moment in every journey where the path widens, where the lessons sink in, and the light dawns anew. This can be something so new it crosses the threshold of the cutting edge, or it can be something ancient that we suddenly remember. When we quiet the mind, there are many memories waiting there like fresh stories to be told. It's like they are waiting for us to pass the test we have assigned ourselves, to cut the bullshit and come see our true selves.

This book has been a journey of remembrance for me, and one of the things I have remembered, by peeling back the layers of illusion, was to step into the cycles of love. The goddess has walked beside us for many lifetimes. She gifts us with treasures such as the moon and her cycles to show us the way, and symbols such as the birds and their songs to show us how to be free and beautiful. She shares stories, breath, and rituals with us, so that we can place them in our own hearts. And again, I remember: Venus is cycling to the pulse of our own hearts.

And with awareness, as I stand here at the threshold of completion, I do not end, I begin again.

We step forward not as seekers searching for what was missing, but as awakened ones who have remembered the truth of who we are and the power that lives within us. I have already started channeling Personone, and it has become clear to me that she is not only the third goddess in the Awakening the Goddess Within series, but also the third goddess representative in the lineage of Rose Heart, an ancient mystery school and magenta light code lineage that passes through the portal Venus creates in the sky to Earth.

And so, as I move forward in time channeling these books, a second layer of meaning is coming through about this lineage and mystery school. My awareness has opened up further, from beginning as a fully embodied high priestess of the goddess to also an initiate of the Rose Heart Line, and I think you will see these themes come more fully alive in the future books. For now, I do not know too much, but here is a structural understanding that is as loose as the threads of a spider's web and so can be changed in the softest of breezes.

The Five-Fold Pathway to Awakening the Goddess Within

1. ***Awakening Lilith: Reclaiming the Shadow & the Untamed Feminine***

Lilith is the first initiation, the descent into the primal, raw, and unfiltered aspects of the self. She is the fierce gatekeeper of the underworld, the sacred rebel who refused to lie beneath anyone. Lilith is not the villain of the old stories, she is the one who dared to say no. To awaken Lilith is to awaken your truth, no matter how inconvenient or wild it may seem. She is the pulse in your rage, the clarity in your grief, the spark of fire that will not be extinguished.

This initiation asks you to confront the shadow, not as something to be feared, but as a sacred mirror. Here, you meet the parts of yourself that have been exiled, your anger, your lust, your power, your voice. You call them back home. Lilith invites you to unshackle from shame, from the need to be pleasing, from the scripts handed down through patriarchy and lineage. This is where you reclaim your body, your boundaries, your full emotional range.

In the descent of Lilith, you may feel alone, but you are never truly alone. Thousands of women walk this same spiral with you, reclaiming the wild within. This path teaches you that darkness is fertile ground. That the underworld is not a place of punishment but a womb of rebirth. You are not broken, you are becoming.

To initiate with Lilith is to say: I will no longer abandon myself. It is the beginning of your return to wholeness. From this place of truth and fire, you rise, not polished or perfect, but whole, holy, and unapologetically alive.

I have already written a channeled book called Awakening Lilith in which I did not know that I was calling through the Rose Heart Pathway until the very moment of writing this, so I will have to go back and add a whole chapter about it at some point. But the book itself will be very activating.

2. Embodying Aphrodite: Living as Love, Pleasure, & Radiance.

Aphrodite is the second initiation, the call to return to yourself as love incarnate. She arrives like sunlight warming your skin after a long winter. Not to be chased, but to be received. She is not merely the goddess of romance or beauty; she is the sovereign queen of embodiment. She teaches us that love is not a longing, it is our native language, our most primal truth.

To walk with Aphrodite is to soften the walls around your heart, to let yourself be touched by life again. It is to awaken your senses as sacred instruments: to savor a piece of fruit, to feel the caress of silk on skin, to let music move you without apology. Pleasure becomes holy in her temple, and the body is no longer a battleground, it becomes the altar.

This initiation unthreads the tight stitching of shame and self-denial. Aphrodite reminds us that to receive is to allow the universe to flow through us. That radiance is not something we perform, it is who we are when we are not dimming ourselves to make others comfortable. She asks us to look into the mirror and see the divine staring back.

To embody Aphrodite is to become magnetic, not because you seek attention, but because you are attuned to your own sacred frequency. Love flows to you and through you. You give, not from depletion, but from overflow. You create, not to prove your worth, but to express your joy. Your life becomes a living prayer of sensual devotion.

This is not about perfection. It is about presence. The tender art of being with yourself fully. In your pleasure. In your grief. In your longing. In your radiance. Aphrodite walks beside you, her rose heart open, whispering, You are already the love you've been seeking.

3. Remembering Persephone: The Sacred Descent, Sovereignty & Inner Alchemy

Persephone represents the sacred turning point, the space between worlds. Neither only light like Aphrodite, nor solely shadow like Lilith, she is the threshold walker. Her story is not just about descent; it is about return. She teaches us that power is not found in avoiding the dark, but in learning to carry the light within it.

To tend to Persephone is to tend to the seasons of our own soul. She is the part of us that has been taken, yet also the part that chooses to stay. In this initiation, we are asked to explore our own relationship with grief, cycles, and rebirth. What parts of ourselves were buried in order to survive? And what wisdom did we gather in the underworld that now longs to bloom in spring?

This stage is not about rushing to the light, but learning to walk with both, the inner winter and the inner awakening. It is where we integrate the wisdom of Lilith and the love of Aphrodite into emotional resilience, compassion, and sovereignty. Persephone is both Maiden and Queen. She reminds us that we are allowed to hold paradox, to be soft and strong, grieving and growing, sacred and human.

To tend her is to reclaim rhythm and reawaken inner balance. She moves with the Earth, with the seasons, and with the soul's deep need for reflection and renewal. Her medicine is slowness, stillness, and the remembering that every descent has a purpose.

We can work with Persephone by honoring our own cycles, tracking our emotional seasons, and creating sacred rituals around transition. The pomegranate seeds in her myth symbolize our soul agreements, the choices we make to stay present with what is hard, knowing it is part of our soul's maturing.

She is the embodiment of inner alchemy. Through her, we become whole. She holds the keys to the underworld not as a victim, but as a sovereign queen who has made peace with the shadows. Her path calls us into deeper emotional intelligence, psychic sensitivity, and compassionate leadership.

This is where the Ascending Venus cycle begins to stir. As Venus prepares to rise from the depths, the priestess too rises, no longer just for herself, but to hold sacred space for others. To walk with Persephone is to prepare for sacred leadership. This is the step between inner transformation and outer embodiment.

When we emerge with Persephone, we are no longer who we were. We have seen the truth of ourselves, and we choose to rise with it. We become the bridge between shadow and light, death and rebirth, winter and spring. We become temple keepers of our own being, ready to hold space for others in devotion, ceremony, and truth.

In this way, Persephone is the gatekeeper of the Rose Heart Priestess Path. She blesses the soil from which the sacred feminine blooms. And in tending her, we tend to the future of the lineage, preparing the heart to rise with Venus into sacred leadership and cosmic remembrance.

4. Reclaiming Magdalene: The Sacred Union & Divine Feminine Mysteries

The Magdalene Codes are not just teachings, they are transmissions, vibrational truths carried through time by those who remembered, even when the world tried to forget. Mary Magdalene was never merely a figure in someone else's story. She was a priestess, a teacher, a healer, a keeper of the Rose Mysteries. Her lineage, woven with the wisdom of Sophia, the holy wisdom of the divine feminine, holds the codes of sacred union, not only between man and woman but between soul and form, between light and shadow, between heaven and earth.

To walk this path is to remember that the body is not separate from spirit. That love is not something we fall into, but something we become. This is the deepest of initiations, the merging of duality into divine oneness. Through the Magdalene path, we begin to see that sacred union is not about another completing us; it is about dissolving the illusion of separation within ourselves.

In sacred union, the inner masculine is no longer dominant or distorted by control, nor is the inner feminine bound by silence or sacrifice. Instead, the two aspects meet in balance. The masculine offers presence, protection, structure, and clarity. The feminine offers intuition, creativity, flow, and feeling. Together, they form the sacred chalice of creation, the holy grail within each of us.

This is not a philosophy to be studied but an experience to be embodied. When you walk the Magdalene path, you are asked to tend to your body as a temple. To let your breath be prayer. To allow intimacy, with self, others, and the divine, to be your teacher. This path often calls forth deep healing, especially in areas where love has been distorted by fear, where sexuality has been shamed, or where vulnerability has been mistaken for weakness.

You may find that as you work with these codes, old memories resurface, not only from this life, but from past lives, ancestral patterns, and collective pain. You may feel the grief of the feminine silenced across centuries... and also the strength that survived it. This is the power of the Magdalene path, it brings everything up to be alchemized in the heart, the seat of true union.

On this path, tantra becomes sacred, not as something overtly sexual, but as the weaving of energy and presence, the merging of matter and spirit. Pleasure is reclaimed as a doorway to presence. Devotion becomes embodied. And every act, cooking, dancing, resting, making love, speaking truth, becomes an offering.

For many, this path also activates the codes of divine

service. As you walk in union within yourself, your very presence becomes healing to others. You may feel called to teach, to guide, to create sacred containers where others can remember who they are. You may become a living temple of love, radiating the Magdalene frequency simply by being who you are.

And this is the point of the Magdalene Codes: not to become her, but to awaken her within. The Christed Feminine lives in you. The Divine Masculine walks beside her. Together, they rise, not to conquer, but to create.

This is the final petal of the Rose Heart Pathway, but in truth, it is just the beginning. For once sacred union has been remembered, the way we live, love, and lead changes forever.

You are not here to repeat the old stories.
You are here to write new ones, with your heart wide open.
You are not here to search for wholeness.
You are here to reveal it, live it, embody it.
You are not here to wait for the return of the goddess.
She has already returned, through you.

5. Reinventing Isis: Alchemy, Rebirth, & the Cosmic Womb

The final initiation of the Rose Heart Pathway returns us to the Great Mother, the divine architect of resurrection, healing, and magic. Isis is the weaver of life and death, the breath between worlds, the silent hum of eternity pulsing through all things. She is the womb of the cosmos itself, the void that births stars, the intelligence that holds together what has been broken, the magic that resurrects what was lost and makes it whole again.

To awaken the Rose Codes of Isis is to step into the sacred art of energetic mastery. This is not the magic of illusion, it is the alchemy of remembrance. Isis reminds us that we are not powerless participants in our lives; we are co-creators, deeply connected to the rhythms of nature and the divine architecture of the universe. She does not ask us to escape our humanity, she asks us to claim it as holy.

This path is one of deep maturity and sovereignty. It is not about control, but alignment. It is about remembering that our thoughts, emotions, words, and actions are spells, and that we are casting reality with every breath. Isis teaches us how to become conscious of this process, how to speak with intention, how to move with grace, how to harness the raw matter of the unseen and give it form.

To walk with Isis is to remember your own power of rebirth. Like the myth where she gathers the scattered pieces of Osiris and breathes life into him once more, we too are gathering the lost parts of ourselves, the forgotten gifts, the fragmented memories, the silenced voices, and breathing life into our wholeness. This is not a surface-level resurrection. This is soul-level restoration. It is a rebirth into your original frequency, your divine design.

Isis is also the guardian of the Cosmic Womb, the space where all possibilities reside. In her temple, there is no rushing, no forcing. There is trust in divine timing, in sacred cycles, in gestation. We are reminded that everything that is meant to bloom must first be rooted. Everything that is meant to rise must first be held.

As this initiation unfolds, you may find yourself called to deeper rituals, to sacred silence, to time in nature, to ceremonies of light and shadow. You may be called to serve as a midwife of consciousness, helping others birth their own becoming. Or you may simply be called to rest, to return to the womb and be held in the mystery before rising again.

Whatever your expression, this path is the embodiment

of High Priestess energy. It is not a title, it is a frequency. One that whispers: you remember. One that says: you have always known.

The Isis codes live in your bones. They are the blueprints of your becoming. As you reclaim them, you step into your full power, not as someone who needs to be more, but as someone who has come home.

This is the end of the spiral, and it is also the beginning.

You are not broken, you are sacred.

You are not forgotten, you are eternal.

You are not separate, you are the womb of the world.

I have not yet written these last three books, and so things may become clearer and more entangled. And the birth of this version of the Rose Heart lineage will come into being. Aphrodite, Inanna, Venus, she has many names, but one truth. She is love, not as an emotion but as a force, as a living, breathing current that moves through all things. Her lessons are not learned in books alone, but in the body, in the breath, in the choices we make each day. The rose is her symbol, and within it lies the mystery of the path. The spiral unfurls from the center, always expanding, always returning to itself. This is the journey we have taken. This is the journey of every soul who dares to step into the full expression of love.

This spiral is not linear, it is feminine, expansive, multidimensional. It invites us not to rush, but to feel. Not to conquer, but to remember. This is not a path of perfection, but of presence.
We are not here to remain small, afraid of our own divinity. We are not here to shrink from our desires, to silence our voices, to live in separation from what calls us home. We are here to embody love, to awaken to the truth that we are already whole, that we have always been whole.

Karma is not punishment. It is the imprint of past creation, the energy we have set into motion. It is the spiral we move through, and it is ours to unravel. Every moment of conscious love dissolves what was once bound. Every act of deep presence rewrites the story. Every time we choose to love instead of fear, to soften instead of harden, to trust instead of close, we shift the collective story. That is the power of one heart aligned with Source.

This is why we receive as much as we give. This is why we honor beauty. This is why we breathe, why we soak in the sea, why we listen to the wind, why we chant AUM and feel the vibrations move through our bones. These are not small things. These are the keys to unlocking everything.

To live as a priestess, as an embodiment of Aphrodite's essence, is to engage with the sacred in all things. It is to know that love is not passive, it is the most powerful force in the universe. And when we live in alignment with love, in harmony with the cycles of giving and receiving, we are not just healing ourselves, we are healing the world.

We become the ones who walk with intention, who create sacred spaces in the ordinary moments, who remember the divine in a single breath.
This is the embodiment of the Rose Heart.

We are no longer bound to the old stories unless we choose to be. We are no longer required to walk the paths of suffering, to repeat patterns that no longer serve us. We are free. This is the ultimate gift of Aphrodite, the realization that love is liberation. That pleasure is not sin, but a guidepost back to ourselves. That beauty is not superficial, but the language of the divine. That to love ourselves fully, wholly, without condition, is the most sacred act we can ever perform. It is not just permission, it is a reclamation. A resurrection of what has always been holy.

There is a call echoing through the hearts of women, a remembering that is rising from the depths of time itself. The lineage of the Rose Heart, the sacred feminine path that has existed since the earliest priestess traditions, is awakening once more. It has never truly been lost, only dormant, waiting for the moment when consciousness would be ready to receive it again. That time is now. The temple is no longer made of stone. It is made of breath. Of words. Of moments of sacred choice. And you, beloved one, are its living flame.

Across the world, in whispers and waves, in rituals and revelations, women are stepping into their ancient power. We are reclaiming the teachings once buried beneath the sands of forgotten temples, coded in myths, bones, bloodlines, and dreams. We are remembering that we are not separate from the divine, we are the embodiment of it. The goddess does not live outside of us; she breathes within us. She stirs in our blood, speaks through our intuition, moves through our dance, and reawakens through our sacred remembering. Her pulse is the beat of our hearts. Her knowing is the fire in our wombs. Her presence is our presence.

This is the essence of the Rose Heart lineage, the path of embodied love, divine sovereignty, and cosmic remembrance. To walk this path is not simply to honor the goddess in ritual, but to live her truth in every breath. It is to become the living temple. It is to be love incarnate, to create beauty unapologetically, to stand tall in the fullness of one's radiance, and to move through the world as both blessing and beacon. It is to walk with roses in our hair and fire in our bellies. It is to embrace the paradox of softness and strength, sensuality and wisdom, chaos and creation, not as contradictions, but as the whole of what it means to be divine feminine.

The Five-Fold Pathway to Awakening the Goddess Within is emerging now, rising like sacred geometry from the heart of Gaia herself. As more women remember, reawaken, and rise into the roles of High Priestess, Oracle, Mystic, and embodied guide, the spiral calls us deeper. This is not a linear journey, it is a spiral of initiation, a living dance with shadow and light, descent and ascension. It is the path of remembrance, of reclamation, and of radiant power. This sacred spiral aligns with the celestial rhythm of Venus, whose dance across the heavens traces a perfect five-petaled rose, a pentagram inscribed not by human hands, but by the cosmos itself. A living symbol of the goddess. A message written in the stars.

We are not just watching the rise of the goddess, we are the rise. We are the ones reweaving the myths, rebirthing the temples, and restoring love as the law of life. The Rose Heart is not a metaphor. It is a living lineage. And now, dear one, you are being called to walk it.

These five steps are not linear, they are a spiral, a continuous unfolding that deepens with each cycle of Venus, with each turn of the great celestial dance. This path is reawakening now because we are ready. The consciousness of the planet is shifting, and the goddess is returning through the hearts of women who dare to remember. Not remember with the mind alone, but with the body, the breath, the soul's knowing.

As Venus traces her radiant pentagram in the heavens, she marks sacred phases of descent and ascent, mirroring our own spiritual journeys. Her dance is not random, it is encoded with deep cosmic intelligence, a pattern that reminds us that every fall leads to a rise, that every ending is a portal to rebirth. The current generation of priestesses is aligning with these Venus star points, bringing forth teachings that have been hidden beneath the veils of time, ready now to be revealed again in a new light.

Across the world, new temples are rising, not always built of stone, but of intention and energy. Sisterhood circles are gathering under moonlight. Mystery schools are opening in kitchens and forests, on beaches and in bedrooms, wherever women remember that the sacred has never left us. We are not reviving something dead, we are reactivating something eternal.

Ancient texts, from the Hymns of Inanna to the Nag Hammadi scriptures, whisper of these very same spirals, myths of resurrection, descent, transformation, and divine union. The Emerald Tablets of Thoth, the Sophia Pistis, and the Gnostic gospels speak of the sacred feminine as the bridge between the earthly and celestial realms. Even the Orphic Mysteries of ancient Greece revered Venus as the weaver of souls, the harmonizer of fates. These weren't stories meant to be worshipped from afar. They were maps. Keys. Codes waiting to be unlocked in the living body.

And now, we are the ones holding those keys. This is not a return to the past, but an evolution of it. The priestesses of today are not tasked with imitation, but with embodiment. We are not here to replicate the old ways, we are here to renew them through our lived expression, to weave the ancient with the modern in ways that serve this moment in time, this version of Earth's awakening.

The Rose Heart lineage lives not only in sacred chants and temple walls but in the quiet choices we make each day to love ourselves, to see the sacred in the mundane, to speak truth even when our voice trembles, to trust the spiral when all logic tells us to run. We carry the temple within us now. We are the altar. We are the offering. We are the flame.

We are stepping into a time when the goddess is not only remembered, but lived. Where the sacred and the ordinary are no longer separate. Where devotion is not limited to ritual, but infused in how we speak, how we breathe, how we rise each morning and meet the world with tenderness and power. This is the way of Aphrodite, the way of Inanna, of Isis, of Mary Magdalene. This is the way of the rose. The way of love as liberation.

And so, as we close this book, we do not close the journey. We step forward, not with certainty, but with devotion. With the rose in our hands and the spiral beneath our feet. We remember that we are love. That we are whole. That we are, and have always been, divine.

Reference

Books and Academic Sources

Baring, A., & Cashford, J. (1991). The myth of the goddess: Evolution of an image. Penguin Books.

Copenhaver, B. P. (1992). Hermetica: The Greek Corpus Hermeticum and the Latin Asclepius in a new English translation, with notes and introduction. Cambridge University Press.

Eliade, M. (1958). The sacred and the profane: The nature of religion. Harcourt, Brace & World.

Freke, T., & Gandy, P. (2001). The Jesus mysteries: Was the "original Jesus" a pagan god? Three Rivers Press.

George, A. R. (1999). The epic of Gilgamesh: The Babylonian epic poem and other texts in Akkadian and Sumerian. Penguin Classics.

Harrison, J. E. (1903). Prolegomena to the study of Greek religion. Cambridge University Press.

Hesiod. (c. 700 BCE). Theogony.

Homer. (c. 8th century BCE). Iliad.

Jacobsen, T. (1976). The treasures of darkness: A history of Mesopotamian religion. Yale University Press.

Kramer, S. N. (1963). The Sumerians: Their history, culture, and character. University of Chicago Press.

Pagels, E. (1979). The Gnostic gospels. Random House.

Penglase, C. (1994). Greek myths and Mesopotamia: Parallels and influence in the Homeric hymns and Hesiod. Routledge.

Sacks, D. (1995). Encyclopedia of the ancient Greek world. Facts on File.

Sered, S. S. (1994). Priestess, mother, sacred sister: Religions dominated by women. Oxford University Press.

West, M. L. (1997). The East face of Helicon: West Asiatic elements in Greek poetry and myth. Oxford University Press.

Wilson, B., & Jacobovici, S. (2014). The lost gospel: Decoding the ancient texts that reveal Jesus' marriage to Mary Magdalene. Pegasus Books.

Ancient Texts and Primary Sources

Hymn to Inanna. (c. 2100 BCE). Sumerian Text.

The Epic of Gilgamesh. (c. 1800 BCE). Mesopotamian Text.

Ugaritic Texts. (c. 1400 BCE). Canaanite Texts.

Web Sources

Alison, & Don. (n.d.). Sacred Destinations: Aphrodite's temples and myths. Sacred Destinations. Retrieved from https://www.alisonanddon.com

Earth Storiez. (n.d.). Aphrodite in mythology and ancient traditions. Earth Storiez. Retrieved from https://www.earthstoriez.com

Kyprios Character. (n.d.). Aphrodite and Cyprus: The goddess's cultural influence. Kyprios Character. Retrieved from https://kyprioscharacter.eie.gr

Lithub. (n.d.). The myths of Aphrodite and their evolution. Lithub. Retrieved from https://www.lithub.com

Mylifetea. (n.d.). The symbolism of doves in Aphrodite worship. Mylifetea. Retrieved from https://www.mylifetea.com

Nostos. (n.d.). Ancient Greek temples and rituals of Aphrodite. Nostos. Retrieved from https://www.nostos.com

OwlCation. (n.d.). Aphrodite's influence on later goddess traditions. OwlCation. Retrieved from https://www.owlcation.com

Periodicos UFPB. (n.d.). Academic journal articles on goddess worship. Periodicos UFPB. Retrieved from https://periodicos.ufpb.br

Rebecca Holly. (n.d.). The resurgence of the divine feminine and Aphrodite's archetype. Rebecca Holly. Retrieved from https://www.rebeccaholly.com.au

Ritual Cape Cod. (n.d.). Aphrodite's sacred rites and modern interpretations. Ritual Cape Cod. Retrieved from https://www.ritualcapecod.com

Reiki Rachael. [@reikirachae]. (2025, 3, 21). Equinox Energy Activation [Video]. YouTube.

https://youtu.be/Mj7H4sutKUo?si=NkVm-XqelUKH5skC

Vice. (n.d.). Ancient love spells and Aphrodite's influence on modern witchcraft. Vice. Retrieved from https://www.vice.com

Wikipedia. (n.d.). Aphrodite. Wikipedia. Retrieved from https://en.wikipedia.org/wiki/Aphrodite

Gratitude

A Heartfelt Thank You

Thank you for walking this spiral of remembrance with me. This book was born from a love of learning, guided by the wisdom streams of Sophia, the radiant heart of Hathor, and the timeless presence of the Goddess in all her forms. Each page has been woven with care, with many hours spent researching, fact-checking, and channeling truth through both herstory and soul.

If this book touched something within you, I would be deeply grateful if you would leave an honest review on Amazon. Your words ripple outward, helping others discover this work and letting me know that these transmissions are landing where they're most needed.

Every review is a blessing, allowing me to continue creating and offering more of this sacred work.

Thank you for your presence.

Thank you for remembering.

May the codes of light continue to bloom within you.

With love and devotion,

Sofia Hator xx

About the Author

Step into the sacred frequency of Sofia Hathor, a spiritual oracle and vessel for the divine feminine. As a devoted channel for goddess energy, Sofia receives and transmits sacred texts and soul activations that support the next wave of goddess remembrance on Earth.

With a heart rooted in the Rose Lineage and a voice guided by Sophia wisdom and Hathorian light, Sofia bridges ancient codes with modern awakening. Her writings serve as portals—reawakening the sacred, the sensual, the sovereign feminine within every reader.

Through her books, transmissions, and oracle work, Sofia invites you into a world where the spiral is sacred, the body is a temple, and love is the law of life. Her words are not just read—they are felt. They stir the soul, awaken the womb, and open the path of remembrance.

Join Sofia Hathor on this sacred journey. Let the goddess rise within you. Let the ancient truths speak once more through your own becoming.

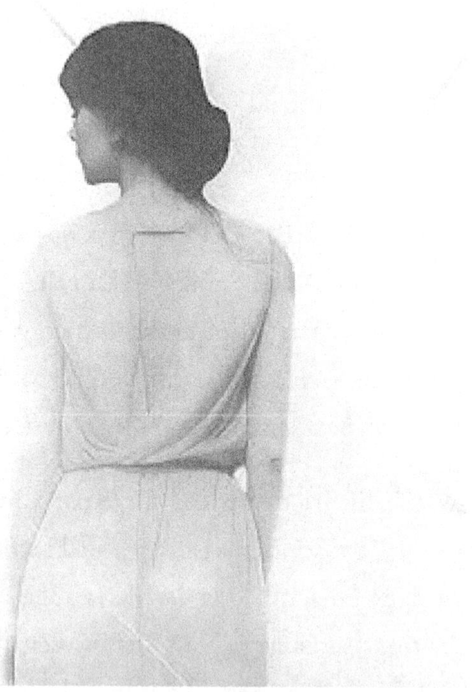

Printed in Great Britain
by Amazon

61490885R00087